Why Not?

Quantity discounts are available on bulk orders.
Contact info@TAGPublishers.com for more information.

TAG Publishing, LLC
2618 S. Lipscomb
Amarillo, TX 79109
www.TAGPublishers.com
Office (806) 373-0114
Fax (806) 373-4004
info@TAGPublishers.com

ISBN: 978-1-59930-405-2

First Edition

Why Not?

Your Best Years Are Yet to Come

Attila Varga

I dedicate this book to all those that I had the pleasure of knowing over the years. I want to specifically acknowledge my wonderful family, my parents and brother, my friends, teachers, mentors, and all those that influenced me over the years. You all played a key role in the person I have become and for that I thank you very much.

About the Author

Attila Varga is an internationally recognized leadership trainer, speaker, and executive success coach. He works with individuals who seek fulfillment and success as well as with corporations looking to enhance and leverage their human capital to excel.

Attila's background includes nearly two decades of management experience in the Captial Markets division of global financial institutions. He is a Chartered Financial Analyst and received his Executive MBA from the Richard Ivey School of Business.

Attila provides his clients with the tools and techniques necessary to utilize the principles of success and progression. He specializes in the gap between knowing and doing that exists in large organizations and within each individual, and teaches how to go from existing to excelling both in business endeavours and personal relationships. Attila's teaching transforms his clients thinking by raising their awareness of the infinite potential and creativity of the human mind. Attila re-energizes the organizations and people he consults with, creating enthusiasm and passion for achieving corporate and personal objectives. His clients see real measurable improvement in their results in every area. The benefits he offers include an improved corporate culture, focused on execution of strategy; effective change management; and innovation.

Contents

Foreword

Attila Varga knows the power of belief and vision. Years ago, as a Hungarian refugee in a new country where he didn't speak the language, Attila dared to create a new life brimming with opportunities. Yet even with all the wonderful experiences he encountered as he matured and changed, he soon reached a point in his life where he wondered, "Is this all there is?" Attila committed himself to finding the answer and this book documents that journey as he discovered that not only was there more, his best was yet to come!

October 21, 2011 will mark 50 years from the day I picked up a copy of Napoleon Hill's classic, *Think and Grow Rich*. I've been a serious student of the mind and have spent virtually all of my adult life studying human behavior: why we do the things we do and don't do some of the things we know will bring us better results. We have deep reservoirs of potential lying dormant within and all we need is the key to unlock it. *Why Not?* is that key.

We all want to explore our dreams and live an abundant life but so many become complacent and accept the status quo. Attila is an outstanding example of what's possible when you make an irrevocable decision to step out of your comfort zone and go after what you want. Most people go after what they think they can achieve, as opposed to what they really want.

It was reported that President John F. Kennedy would have his speeches written so that a 10 year old could understand them; he was an extremely effective communicator. Attila too has also mastered the skill of conveying complex ideas in a simple way so virtually everyone can grasp the ideas and benefit from them.

Attila has done a wonderful job blending concepts and principles that will help you on your path of self discovery with examples of how these same strategies positively affected his own life.

Why Not? will help you understand how to overcome obstacles, free yourself from the past, and move forward faster and farther than you ever thought possible. It all starts with a decision - one decision - to start seeing that change right away.

Bob Proctor,
Teacher in The Secret
and bestselling author of
You Were Born Rich

Chapter 1

The Hamster Wheel

Why Not?

Chapter 1
The Hamster Wheel

One morning a few years ago, I was going about my usual morning routine. I'd just showered and gone to the mirror to shave. I noticed the gray at my temples and my wayward eyebrows. They stuck out in all directions like long antennas. I leaned closer and noticed the bags under my eyes, the imperfections of my skin, my receding hair line and my well rounded figure. None of these physical attributes were new. I had seen them all many times before, but it never really sank in how quickly time had flown by.

In my heart, I was still in my early twenties, but the mirror showed something quite different. I was about forty at the time and the passage of years showed on my face and body. I can't say that I was happy with how my body changed, but what really troubled me was what happened inside – I was very unhappy. Each day was drudgery and somehow my hopes and dreams were fading away.

Nothing really changed that morning from a physical perspective. I only became increasingly aware of my dissatisfaction with my life as the day went along. I noticed things that I paid no attention to previously and, to be honest, couldn't have cared less about before. But now things felt wrong. A lot of confusing feelings and thoughts ran through my mind and they surprised me.

The strong feelings of dissatisfaction were hard to describe, I didn't understand why they reared their ugly heads now. Yesterday nothing bothered me, but today it seemed like my life was a mess.

I am a Hungarian-born Canadian and now live in a beautiful suburb of Toronto, halfway between this great city and Niagara Falls. I live what many would consider a charmed life. My home is located in a nice middle class neighbourhood where neighbours know each other and look out for each other. During winter, when the snow covers everything, neighbours get together and help each other dig out. People pitch in and help the elderly, take care of their sidewalks and driveways, as well as the homes of those who happen to be away on vacation or business that week. Everybody has manicured lawns, and flowers are a natural part of landscaping. You would have to look really hard to find garbage anywhere. Flower beds are planted by the city on the main roads, and everywhere you look you see prosperity.

My children go to school in a beautiful park where you can find both the elementary and high school. My three girls, ages sixteen, nine, and seven, walk to school together in the morning and come home together in the afternoon. Everyone knows each other; we have a real sense of community. Sirens can only be heard if there is a car accident. Crime is effectively unknown. It is almost like we live in a bubble. Our life is so different than what I see in the media. On TV and in the papers, we are bombarded with violence, despair and hardship. The whole world has gone mad. The way we live, it's so quiet, peaceful and harmonious. So what could I possibly have to be unhappy about? I didn't understand.

Still wondering what was wrong with me, I went to work. I am a banker by trade. I joined the financial services industry some eighteen years ago and have been working for large global institutions in their capital markets division for the majority of that time. Through hard work and self-education I was able to achieve considerable success and earn a great income. In Canada, the two dominant industries are natural resources and banking. Working for Canada's premier financial institutions in the division that people consider to be the most prestigious should have made me very content, satisfied and generally happy. Yet even that wasn't doing it for me that day.

My commute from home to Bay Street in Toronto, which is like Wall Street in New York, is about an hour. Most people, like me, take the commuter trains while others drive on the Queen Elizabeth Way, one of our main highways. The commuter train is operated by the Government of Ontario and is called the GO. You may think that if it is a government managed business it must be bad, but that is not true in this case. The trains are modern, clean and very comfortable. The rail cars have three levels with lots of comfortable leather covered seats. The service is rather good as well. There are many train lines that bring people in from towns surrounding Toronto into Union Station, which is the center of the downtown core. I am on the Lakeshore line, where the trains are frequent and if I miss my usual one, I don't have to wait too long before the next train pulls in and off we go.

Since I am on the lakeshore line, it literally means that the train follows the shores of Lake Ontario, and as we get close to downtown the view from the train is beautiful. We see the sparkling blue water and the Toronto Skyline, which includes not only many skyscrapers, but also the CN Tower. Until recently, the CN Tower was the world's tallest free standing structure. People visit Toronto from all over the world to see it and I'm treated to that wonderful view each day.

Passengers on these trains are what one would call the 'office crowd.' Pretty much everyone has a post-secondary education with many also having Masters and Doctoral degrees. By people's faces, their manners and attire, one can see that this is a middle to upper class group. So what is it that I don't like again? What am I unhappy about? I still had no answer.

Then I noticed. Everyone always wears black. I jokingly wondered, 'who died?' You see, especially during the colder months, everyone wears cashmere and cotton overcoats. They are comfortable, very stylish and warm, but they are almost exclusively all black. These dark coats are complemented with black leather bags, black shiny shoes and boots as well as black leather gloves. The only colors that are noticeable are the scarfs and colors university students wear. It is like we are all wearing a uniform. The look is the same every day: no excitement, no colors, just the same old everyday uniform.

At the time, I worked in finance in the CFO's office, right around the time when the Credit markets took the whole world into a tail spin. It was a trying time for everyone. Even those who don't work in the investment banking industry can imagine the demand the market turmoil placed on people in financial reporting areas of all businesses – especially banking. This included senior management of our company, the business heads we supported, internal and external auditors, not to mention the various regulatory bodies who all wanted information. They wanted lots of it with very short deadlines. We were under intense scrutiny. The hours were long and working on the weekend was commonplace.

Though it was a difficult time in regard to what was at stake, in a sense it was also very exciting to be in the middle of what was a global concern. I remember when I was young, growing up in a small mining town in Hungary, a friend of mine once said, "I want to live my life in a way that when I grow old and sit on the porch with my grandchild on my lap, I will have something to remember and stories to tell him about." Well, there is no doubt in my mind I will never forget those days and I know that there are many who feel the same way, not only in Toronto but all around the world. There aren't many people anywhere that weren't impacted by the financial turmoil. The only question was by how much or how badly.

Despite all this 'excitement' I became aware that we were working within a routine. We had month ends every month and quarter ends every three months. We knew what reports to create by when, who needed to receive them and what reconciliation we needed to complete by which day. The only change was the content of these various reports and the occasional change in the format of some of the management presentations. I worked in finance for many years prior to this and I never had a problem with the repetitiveness of the role, but now I took notice. What was happening with me? Why had everything in my world turned dull and gray?

During my commute home, I noticed how drained a lot of people looked—like the life had literally been sucked out of them. Many had nervous twitches, as if the weight on their shoulders might break them completely. Some people continue working away on their BlackBerrys or laptops still connected to the office, while many others simply fell asleep, exhausted. It was then that I realized how few people seem to enjoy themselves. Few have any expression of joy or excitement radiating from them. I almost never see anyone smile on that train.

I was one of the many. I had the same feelings and stress, but why? Over the coming days, I paid more attention to what happened around me. While previously I blocked out other people's conversations to focus on what I needed to do, I now observed what people were saying.

I was amazed how ingrained negativity was in all the conversations I heard. Seldom ever did people discuss planning a wonderful venture or excitedly chat about higher goals they wanted achieve. In general, they never looked forward to another joyful day, week, month or year. Something was always wrong with this picture, but I had failed to notice it. Their daily talk centered on the economy, the boss, the company they worked for, the neighbour whose dog barked all night, the friend who betrayed them, or any number of horrible events. I realized my life had become a series of routine tasks with little difference from one day to the next. For a long time, I'd accepted it – hadn't really thought about it, but now I noticed and what I saw wasn't good. Though I realized I wasn't alone, most people live their life the same way, I also knew this was not how I wanted to live.

Others may commute by taking packed subway cars, bumping into strangers as if they are all packed sardines in a can. Those who commute by taking their cars because they don't need to be with others still feel the drudgery, even if they feel a bit more control in their life. They are the ones who are directing their own way; they *feel* in charge and decide what happens in any moment, but at the same time end up bumper to bumper as if sitting in a parking lot.

You take a different path, and get the same result—stress. Then it hit me. I am a hamster on a wheel, going round and round on a never-ending path with no sense of growth or accomplishment, no joy from one day to the next, with nothing exciting to look forward to. What happened? What happened to my dreams? This is not the life I wanted. All I do is sleep, go to work, go home, go to sleep, go to work, go home, go to sleep, pay bills and pay more bills. What about me? When am I going to have fun and have time to enjoy the sun on my face without all the worry? I couldn't have even the simplest pleasure because the responsibility of the mortgage, the car payments, and the kids' education fund all rested on my shoulders. I felt trapped, which is not a good feeling. But what happened? As long as I can remember, I have been generally happy. Now that I have achieved so much and have so much to show for it, I am unhappy with what I have. How could that be? How did I get here?

My Life and Dreams

I clearly remember my childhood in Hungary. We didn't have much by today's Canadian standards, but we were unaware of that fact. My father worked in the coal mines and my mother was a seamstress in a leather goods factory. We lived in a little one bedroom condominium and didn't have a car. We did have a black and white TV that was capable of showing both of the state run television stations. Yes you did read that right. We had the total of two TV stations playing news items and shows almost exclusively from the Communist Bloc countries. Few shows were from the west, but the ones we were allowed to see brought both excitement and confusion into my mind about how different life was on the other side of the Iron Curtain.

Even though we didn't have much material wealth, I was really happy as a child. I loved to play with my friends, ride my bike, and play music. It was wonderful. I had as many square meals a day as I wanted, a roof over my head, a great brother and wonderful, loving parents. I thought that was all I needed, and at that time it was. I remember lying down on the grass with my friends looking up to the sky watching the clouds and their ever changing shapes float by. These were exciting times! My imagination ran wild. The limitlessness of the sky, the openness I had toward life and its endless possibilities were amazing. The blue of the sky was so captivating. We all had big dreams as children. We dreamed about being rich, living our own lives, being in full control and completely settled in with no worries by the time we were thirty. Life was wonderful and we knew that our future was also going to be wonderful. It will be an absolute joy ride.

As a teenager, things were different. Those years were still happy, but much more trying. I was no longer a child, but not yet a man. I still played music and had many friends. We played many concerts in a number of different countries. It was good to travel and see different lands, different habits and cultures.

I noticed people acted and thought differently in some of those places, but didn't understand what it meant. I assumed it was natural that they lived differently than we did, but knew that they were wrong and we were right, so I didn't give it a lot of thought.

Looking back now, I know that we were ignorant and in many ways innocent. I didn't know any better because, like so many other people, I knew only that which I was raised to believe, so I didn't question it as correct. I was a very curious child and loved to read (still do). I studied philosophy and various religious books because I wanted to understand how life works. I was trying to figure out the rules and how to make the most of my life. In high school, I wrote a love story and entered a literary competition. While my writing didn't get any award, it did almost get me expelled from school! My imagination as a teenage boy was rampant and I didn't exercise restraint in my descriptions when it came to conveying the 'loving' part of my story.

Playing music was still a key part of my life as from the age of seven I had attended a state run music school. When I was nineteen, I received a state diploma for the performing arts from our government. I thought things were going great. I had big plans for my life and saw no limitations. I was on a very good track.

In Hungary, joining the army was obligatory once you graduated high school. I, like everybody else, served eighteen months and eventually demobilized, having achieved the rank of corporal. I have to say that being in the army was a bit of a shock compared to my normal way of life. Although, due to my musical background, I was enlisted in the marching band at the nearest army base, the limits and rules our leaders placed on us were difficult to take. I had a strong longing for freedom, but in the army I learned that what I wanted as an individual was no longer relevant. People with more stripes on their sleeves decided when I was going to eat, sleep or do anything.

As you can imagine, it is not one of the better times in my life. But it was a time when I came to a life-changing realization. My body may be locked in a confined space and my actions and activities very limited, but the army couldn't control my thoughts. My mind became my sanctuary. It was a place where my dreams ran wild with no one to tell me what to do or when to do it. Every day I planned what I would do with my life once I demobilized. I imagined all the wonderful things I would achieve and experience and those dreams kept me happy in what was clearly an unhappy situation.

While in the army, it became very clear to me that if I wanted to achieve my dreams, I would need to leave my homeland. From the moment I realized this fact, I knew it would be a difficult thing to achieve.

All my previous travels were within other Communist Bloc countries and, since Hungary was still a Communist society at the time, emigrating from Hungary to western countries directly was not an option. I had to literally escape from my homeland and had to keep my plans a secret. Not even my parents knew about what I had in mind, but it had to be done. I was working as a musician and, on March 15th, 1988, I and a friend of mine left Hungary and escaped to Austria. March 15th has special significance to Hungarians as it is the day when citizens of my country started a revolution to break free from the Habsburg Empire in 1848.

My friend and I felt this was our own personal independence day and we were full of hopes and dreams. We were very nervous, but also extremely excited. We believed in ourselves and decided that whatever happened, we could deal with it and achieve anything we wanted. We headed to Austria and, once over the border, went directly to the capital city of Vienna. What a beautiful city! If you have not yet had the opportunity to visit, I suggest that you put it on your bucket list. In Vienna, we found other Hungarians who escaped prior to us and with their help, entered a refugee camp. The refugee camp was a major eye-opener for me. We were locked up in quarantine for about fourteen days with people from all over the world who had to leave their homeland. Some, like us, had to leave because of other Communist regimes, but there were many others from all kinds of countries who had their own reasons for being there. Interpol officers took pictures of us as well as our finger prints.

They were looking for people who were wanted by other Interpol member countries. Some people were taken away in handcuffs. After the initial fourteen days, we were all moved to *panzios* (motels) across the country while our papers were processed. I was relocated to Windischgarsten, a beautiful ski paradise in the Alps, not too far from Linz. While the town was breathtakingly beautiful and very civilized, the locals didn't like us one bit.

Really, who could blame them? We were all foreigners and had next to nothing. We were put in rooms with up to five other strangers and had neither income nor the ability to work legally. We were given three meals each day and expected to wait until our papers worked their way through the process. Seeing the attitude of the townspeople, the new reality hit me. None of these people were waiting for me; none of these people liked me or were my friends. For them, I contributed nothing and was just a drain on their society. It became painfully obvious that if I wanted a better life, I needed to fit in. I needed to learn how they think, live their life and if I wanted to have a good life myself, then I needed to contribute to society. I realized how different I was in so many ways. I clearly saw that those that have better lives were the ones that contributed more.

People who provided little benefit to society got little back from it. This was a new concept to me since in Hungary everyone had more or less the same lifestyle. A person who worked in the warehouse stocking boxes on top of each other didn't live in a significantly worse situation than the person who was the head of the company. There was no compensation for achievement, so there was no real incentive to do any more than the least you could do.

I believe this is one of the main reasons Communist societies like the one I grew up in couldn't sustain themselves and have had to change so much over the last couple of decades. Austria taught me many lessons about life and had a significant impact on who I am today. My time there forced me to confront many of the ideas I was raised with and realize that I had to make my own path – and that was a very wonderful, if scary, idea.

While I had the opportunity to excel beyond my wildest imagination, there was no more safety net. The government or anyone else was not going to take care of me if something went wrong, so I put it in my mind that I could and would succeed. Throughout this book, I will share lessons I learned with you, as I believe they will help you as well with your everyday lives. But before we move forward, I want to mention that despite all the hardship I experienced, I was generally a very happy man. I knew the day would come when I would travel to the New World and the land of endless opportunities. I had big dreams.

Those dreams and goals kept me happy, even in the midst of very trying situations. My circumstances weren't nearly as important as the hopes I had for who I would become. I dreamed about my future life all the time, awake or sleeping. Finally, one happy day about fourteen months after I left Hungary, I received news from the Austrian government that Canada had accepted me as a landed emigrant and a few short days later I was in Montreal, Canada. I was so giddy I could hardly close my eyes to sleep those first few days. I marvelled at the thought that I was already in the New World. What had been a far off dream while I lay on my army bunk a few short years earlier had come to pass.

I was free—Free to lead an amazing life and make all my dreams come true. To say I was excited is clearly an understatement. Of course, it didn't take long to realize once again that nobody in Canada was waiting for me either and the way people live and think here is different again from what I had experienced in Austria. I clearly didn't fit in and in fact stood out easily in stark contrast to those around me. If I wanted to achieve my dreams, I had to evolve. I needed to become a better version of myself. Shortly after landing in Montreal, I moved to Toronto and started my new life. I was unprepared for this new existence. I had no relatives here, just a couple childhood friends I hadn't seen for years. I spoke almost no English, had only about one thousand dollars and no marketable skills. It was an uphill battle to say the least.

The first several years were very difficult, but I knew what I needed to do: focus on improving myself. I needed marketable skills and I knew that the more I contributed, the better my life would become. I had nothing to speak of, and for quite some time had a negative net worth, but I worked as hard as I could. Although the first several years had a lot of very strong hardships in them, I had my dreams and that kept me happy. I knew I was working toward something wonderful and it was just a matter of time before I was going to achieve my dreams, just as I had achieved my dream of freedom. I didn't know how, and I took many side trips and wrong steps along the way, but I was always heading upward. I imagined myself wealthy and prosperous and believed I could achieve it. I knew it was in me, I believed I could do it even on days and weeks when I had to eat donated food from the church or ate nothing but carrots, as I had no money for anything else.

My intellectual curiosity stayed with me, so naturally I was very keen on educating myself. It is not hard to see how valued knowledge is and how different the lifestyle is of those who have postsecondary education versus those who make their living through manual labour. I had big dreams: I wanted to live in a big house, drive nice cars and have money for anything my heart desired. At the time, I didn't believe that I could start my own business. I didn't have the money, knowledge, or the contacts to get something like that going.

Education and finding a good job with a solid employer was the path I had in mind. University or college years can be some of the best times in anybody's life. It was so good to finally be an adult – and a free one at that. Nobody could tell me what to do anymore. To be finally on my own with other young, excited, hot-blooded young people was awesome.

Finally, I was learning real skills and was on top of the mountain. Pretty much all students have huge plans for their lives, and my imagination kicked into high gear as well. My plan consisted of being married, house paid for by age thirty, driving a sports car and living the dream by age thirty-five. Life would be so good.

All I needed to do is get a good job and, with my smarts and ambition, I thought I'd be the president of a company in no time. At least that was my general belief – and a similar dream seemed to be shared by the students around me. Finding a good job, of course, sometimes isn't quite as easy as one anticipates. In fact, finding a job, any job, may be difficult for some. I can recall how much excitement I had when I landed my first real job in Canada working as an investment advisor. I found working so invigorating. Being in the workforce, and making money just as I imagined, was great. I had so many dreams and goals that I could barely contain myself. When I started working, I had nothing but student loans and a vision of a wonderful, wealthy and very happy life. I worked hard and my personal life was on track as well.

The big day arrived when I made the commitment for better or worse and I knew 'better' was where our lives were headed. My life plan was right on track. I knew nothing could keep me back. Then the news came that I was to be a father and it was the culmination of everything in my life up until that day. Bringing a new life into the world is an experience I can't even verbalize, but I knew my children would have every opportunity and I would work to show them all they could achieve. Within a few years, we had three beautiful girls and I was bursting with pride. I wanted so much for my family, as it was no longer about me and my dream.

It was about *our* dreams and even though the budget was stretched with each new arrival, I worked harder to be sure we had everything we needed to ensure our health and happiness. Having a family changes a lot of things. My individual dreams and desires weren't as important anymore because my focus was on my family. What became important in my mind was to provide for them the best way I could and make sure we had not only the bare necessities, but that we also lived a comfortable, happy life. The transition from my own dreams to providing for my family was a very easy one and I made it willingly.

I loved my family and to take care of them is natural and requires no effort at all. What did take a lot of effort was to figure out how to make the amount of money we needed and make it happen. I, like many others, joined the ranks of the corporate world and put my head down and worked hard. I continued to study at night and got new accreditations, which helped me advance. Then I worked even harder to get increasingly bigger jobs that paid more. After all, we each want growth and advancement in life and financial growth is one way we keep score with ourselves. I wanted to move into a nicer neighbourhood, into a bigger home, drive nicer cars and provide my family better vacations. I wanted to be able to pay for all the things my wife and children desired or needed. It was so easy to finance the expansion of my own expectations through banks and credit arrangements.

I didn't realize that, eventually, all I ended up doing was working to pay off the loans. But even that was okay, I thought, because everybody else lives their life the same way, right? This is how it gets done. We live in an instant gratification society. Anything we want, we can get almost instantaneously. Need information? Go to Google and there it is. Need a mortgage? Go to the bank and get one. Need a new car? Finance it. If I wanted something but didn't have the cash for it, it was no problem because there was always a credit card or credit line available, so let's just get it and figure out how to pay for it later. I think a lot of people can relate to this way of thinking. Even people who are educated in the world of finance can get into this cycle of keeping up with the Joneses.

We live the life we want to live, but get it earlier than we can comfortably afford and finance the rest. It is so very easy to over extend ourselves and that is how we get caught in the trap. We don't even notice and the dreams and desires we once focused on so heavily no longer matter because we must refocus our attention on surviving and making ends meet.

Our longstanding dreams fade away, and instead of focusing on our achievements, we go with the flow and that is exactly what happened to me. Some people find comfort in what they perceive to be safety of a job, even if they don't particularly like what they do.

The reason is that at least the pay check is steady and the bills are paid. Then there are those who are a bit more daring and take jobs that offer some sort of advancement, even if it is not in their ideal field, but they take it because it pays more. In today's economy, job security is no more. We have all seen company reorganizations, restructurings, and the closures of divisions or whole businesses. We all know people who have lost their jobs and seeing their loss of livelihood makes us think. We may not think about it, but subconsciously it instills fear and makes us more risk averse.

We want to protect ourselves and start to compromise without even realizing it. Some even become territorial. I have seen people during my career who were so scared about others knowing things about what they did and how they did it that they put up all kinds of road blocks when implementations or projects affected their area. Fear creeps up on us and becomes part of our everyday life.

I believe most don't even know how much it affects them. Over time, fear joins forces with stress. They make a perfect and very effective couple in convincing us that we don't have choices and have to accept the status quo. The pressure of life builds in small increments. Some years ago, I became conscious of my own level of stress. Sometimes it was as if an elephant sat on my chest and I couldn't breathe. I couldn't pinpoint one cause specifically; it just felt like an avalanche of weight. I observed other people and was amazed to see how common stress is. I noticed that office workers, bus drivers, coffee shop baristas, teachers and even factory workers were completely strained. It wasn't just my job or my situation –everyone else carried around a large load of pressure too. It is very easy to spot anxiety on some people, while others hide it well.

They have a brave face, but it doesn't take long before they open up and show what is underneath. Everybody has stress to some extent, the only question is how much and how well they handle it. While most people, I believe, just accept the pressure they experience in their life as natural, others choose to take pills to ease their pain and anxiety. The boom in the sale of tranquilizer drugs is clear evidence that many want to keep going on rather than deal with the underlying issues. Eventually, years go by and the pressure of life builds up. We all can take it for a while but one day we may wake up and find ourselves incredibly unhappy and that's what happened to me. One day I was fine, the next I was unhappy. There were no big problems or any kind of significant change from one day to the next. One day I was carrying my load like a good little drone and the next I knew I had to change.

Chapter 2
The Rear View Mirror

Why Not?

Chapter 2
The Rearview Mirror

Realizing that I was a hamster on a wheel made me uncomfortable and I needed to know why. I wanted to know why I was not happy when everything looked so good from the outside. We lived such a pleasing life and I thought I was an excellent provider. We had lots of things: we lived in a nice home, drove nice cars, owned a lot of timeshares so we could go on vacations several times every year, and we had considerable savings. For quite some time I thought this should be enough. This is the dream. This is what most people want to achieve with their lives – a comfortable lifestyle and along the way save up for a comfortable retirement so they can look forward to their golden years. This life plan seemed so perfect and well planned that it was natural to want it and I did. I was well on my way, but it still wasn't enough. I needed more. I wanted more money to have complete financial security, but that wasn't the only thing. There was another need – something else that I wanted in my life. The big question then became what that something else might be.

I looked at my life a bit closer and considered what happened to me over the years and how I had progressed toward my goals. I realized a number of things. The first was that at this stage, I didn't really have any real goals of my own anymore. I wanted what everyone else seemed to want. I wanted to be happy and have peace of mind. These sounded like really good goals since everybody I spoke to told me that is what they want too. I thought I must be right because we all want that, so my problem must lie somewhere else – or so I thought. The second thing I realized was what it all means. Although we were doing OK, I hadn't made any meaningful progress in my career recently. I had been on the same level in my company for a number of years and my income was more or less the same as it had been for at least five years. I had plateaued in my career - but why? I knew I was smart and even tried various roles within my company, but I always ended up in the same place. It was as if I had hit a ceiling but couldn't figure out why. I had to wonder, is this it? Is this all I will ever become or achieve? Am I done growing?

All kinds of questions came to my mind as I thought about my situation. I wondered if I had it in me to move up or if I had maxed out my own level of competence. Was I good enough to get more? It didn't seem like it because, despite my trying, I was just not moving forward. It was strange because there was a strong sense within that I had a lot more to offer. I was absolutely puzzled. Something just didn't add up. I reasoned that I must be in the wrong place. Others seem to be getting better opportunities to advance themselves. There were junior people who had passed me by. I didn't believe they were smarter than me. I reasoned that they must have gotten lucky breaks. How else could it make sense?

The idea of being at the right place at the right time became big part of my focus. I thought that one day, my new boss would realize how great I am and give me that long awaited promotion. But what if it didn't happen? Could I just go from team to team and start over repeatedly? Did I want to keep on trying or was this my destiny? I was only about halfway through my life and if this was it, if there was no more progression or growth then what am I going to do? How would I keep myself happy? I was convinced that I was a good person, very smart and capable. There was so much in me to give, but opportunities weren't coming my way. Also, there was a great deal of competition in the work place and people aren't always friendly. At times, office politics took center stage and the focus shifted from moving things forward to making it through.

There were people trying to gain power and influence, often at the expense of others. We all know how much more teams achieve when there is a group focus and everyone works toward a common goal. Yet all too often, people tend to push their own agenda ahead no matter what. Looking back over my years in the workforce, there aren't many examples of my managers taking consistent and effective steps in building a team mentality, either. As a manager myself, I could have done a much better job in many areas. We all know how important it is to work as a team. While working for a big Canadian bank, I had the pleasure of attending a function where our new Chief Operating Officer was the keynote speaker. He is a Canadian by birth, and spent years in London, England working for large multinational organizations in increasingly larger roles before returning to Canada to take on this very senior position. He is by all means a very impressive individual. During his presentation, he said a few things that had a profound impact on me and I will never forget them. The essence of his message included a few simple points.

He said, "During my career I have all too often seen teams not working toward the common goal. I want you to know that I have zero patience for that."

Wow, I thought, this is impressive and he is making the rules of the 'game' very clear. He got everyone's attention.

He continued, "I want you to picture the rowing competition between Oxford and Cambridge. Both teams have young, very athletic and capable members. They all sit in their boats waiting for the starting gun to go off. The spectators are full of excitement and the race begins. In one of the boats each member pulls their paddle with the same intensity, with the same rhythm, with all the power they have going in the direction of the finish line. In another boat while some of the team members give their very best others simply keep their paddle out of the water. Even worse, some paddle in the opposite direction. Now, which team do you think will win?" I could not have been more impressed with this example. Everyone got the message as it was very clear and very powerful. I just wish everyone in the organization had heard this, understood it, and worked by this powerful thought. Office politics are alive and well in every company. Hearing the COO was very motivational and made an impact on me as well as my coworkers.

After the presentation, we all went back to our desks and continued with the routine of the day. But with this new mental picture planted in my mind, I noticed how many areas and situations I experienced where I had seen people paddling in different directions. My awareness rose considerably. Behaving this way was very commonplace and frustrating. It was so clear that there is a better way, but so few people were doing it. I had to wonder if this was normal. The thought crossed my mind that this perhaps is the way people are and maybe I should just accept that and get on with things. But what does accepting it mean? Is this how I will always live my life? Will I always be in these kinds of environments? Will I always be working in places where people constantly wrong me and each other? Is this how it is going to be all the time? A lot of people have questions like this going through their mind as they try to make sense of their lives.

The pressure increases day-by-day, taking a large toll on our mental and physical well-being. Around the age of forty, after about twenty years of working in this environment, physical and mental illnesses manifest in our bodies. Some people get high blood pressure, headaches, back pains, cancer and all kinds of other diseases while others are diagnosed with depression or chronic anxiety requiring medication and/or counselling. Fear about our future starts to kick in and as we evaluate where we are and compare that to where we thought we'd be. This could be sobering and results in many of us became very conservative. We become less and less willing to try new things. Making any type of change becomes very difficult. We feel a strong need to protect what we have achieved or accumulated. This, of course, is a vicious cycle simply because the only thing that remains the same is the fact that things are always changing. By standing still and trying to protect everything, you actually fall behind. I have seen so many people that had difficulty moving forward and this is especially evident in the working world. Over the years, as I watched or participated in reorganizations, new initiatives or evolutions in the companies I worked for, it always seemed like a forced change – not something that people looked forward to or welcomed. I know you have all heard the saying "You can't teach and old dog new tricks." It seems to be a true statement, but only because we make it so. But it doesn't have to be that way.

When looking for the answers to our life questions, it is easy to start blaming others for our situation and the way we feel. We begin looking for the reasons in our past. We recall all the people who wronged us, all the people that took advantage of us. We remember the bad bosses, the things people told us that made us feel bad or inferior. There are so many examples of negative influences in our lives that we sometimes wonder how we even got this far.

Simply listening to what people around me were talking about showed me how many people live in the past. I heard people complain about what happened only minutes ago all the way to what happened in their childhood. I heard complaints about friends who betrayed, teachers who didn't care, parents who didn't allow something to happen, and neighbours who, blah blah blah – the list goes on. No matter who was telling the story, everything was always wrong and it was always somebody else's fault. I was no different in my own words and thoughts, but I hadn't realized it. Speaking that way seemed a natural thing to do. I remember going to lunch meetings with people, out for a few drinks after work with friends or simply being around others and the dominant conversation in most of these situations was complaints about all the bad things that are going on and how wrong certain people are. These references were usually weighted toward the managers or the decision-makers. If anyone else had been listening, it would have sounded like none of these higher ups know what they were doing.

Then there are people who just like disliking others. At times, they snapped and found an enemy who drove them crazy. I have seen instances when people disliked someone even without knowing this person. They never had a meeting and never spoke to each other, yet there was this strong feeling of hatred. They believed that this person wronged them or was the cause of whatever their challenges, and would hold onto this grudge for the rest of their lives. You have probably heard something similar yourself when someone said that 'so and so did something and I will never let them off the hook, I will never forgive them for what they did.' Somehow, people have a sense of relief when they have someone's shoulder to cry on, somebody to share their difficulties with.

It is almost like a confession; sharing the problem with someone else transfers the problem to that other person so they no longer carry the full load. It is now partially this other person's problem as well. Negative thoughts automatically fly through our minds and convince us that this is a dangerous, unforgiving and ruthless life. I was so convinced that I was a good man, I did everything I could and it most certainly was not my fault if something went wrong. It was always somebody else who, whether they realized it or not, wronged me. And if they didn't wrong me, then the circumstances were just not right. The problem was never with me – or so I thought. I was always right and the problem was everyone else. I find that few people have the courage and the strength to question their own actions. Introspection and self-examination are hard concepts and you tend to uncover things about yourself that you may not like. Once you do, you know you have to change.

Few people are ready to make a change in their personality or in their actions. Those who do realize that they need to change often give it a try – but not a wholehearted try. They will usually 'try' by doing the same thing as before. Then they get the same results and fall back into the same old negativity, blaming everyone else instead of finding out how to really grow and make lasting change in their lives. As I became aware of these common behaviours, I noticed how negative I was, even though I never thought of myself as a negative person, I'd really been happy most of my life. But now I noticed I also had negative thoughts in my mind most of the time. I easily justified and rationalized bad things in my life by blaming others or the circumstances.

The sad part is that I didn't just think negative thoughts, I also said many of them out loud, sharing this negativity. I thought it made me feel better to share and I didn't realize for a long time how wrong I was. I didn't realize by putting all that negativity out into the world and my environment, I was at the same time creating the negativity that came back into my life. You see, what you put out, you attract, so, in reality, I caused all the bad events in my life. I caused all the bad feelings by choosing the negative. I was looking backward to the past with an eye on the negative.

I was holding me back. To describe what I mean by living in the past, I would like to use the analogy of driving a car. As we sit in the driver's seat behind the steering wheel, we have a large clear windshield in front of us. It allows us to look forward and keep an eye on where we are going. We then have a small little mirror in the middle of that windshield that allows us to look backward. The primary purpose of this rear view mirror is to see or notice emergency vehicles catching up with us or to be aware of other vehicles fast approaching from the rear.

We spend about the first third of our life driving along, eyes on the road ahead, for the most part, with the occasional glance at the rear view. Somewhere along the way our attention shifts. After life slaps us around a little bit and we encounter a few step backs, we don't try to learn how to drive better or pay as much attention to what is coming ahead. Instead, we focus on looking backward.

As we sit in our imaginary car, all too often there is no steering wheel anymore; we are no longer driving to our destination because we are caught up in what might have, could have or should have happened in the past. We have converted that wide open clear windshield into a full rear view and have left only a small space to see the road before us. The moment I realized I was doing this, I knew exactly where the problem was. It is painfully obvious how inappropriate it would be to drive our car with the windshield acting as the rear view mirror but for some strange reason, many of us live our lives this way – even if we started out with beautiful dreams.

I woke from the deep, hypnotic-like state I had been in for years and became aware of my own thoughts and actions on a daily basis. As with any learning or growth that takes place, awareness is key and is the first step toward change. Being conscious of my own thoughts and actions allowed me to, over time, regain control of what was going on in my mind and what direction I took. There was a direct link between what I thought and how I felt. Those negative, backward-looking thoughts drained and impacted every aspect of my life and increased my stress. It became painfully obvious that I was causing my own misery. When this realization came, it brought with it a memory that showed me that this knowledge was available to me for some time. I'd heard the words and explanations before, but didn't really understand and internalize their true meanings and so didn't make any change as a result.

Some ten years ago I joined Merrill Lynch in the CFO office. The first few years were absolutely amazing. Everyone loved to work for the Bull. There was camaraderie and everyone wanted to succeed. It was a great environment to be a part of. In the early 2000's, the company had a lot on the go. We were divesting the private client division to another Canadian bank, we had a lot of reorganizations taking place and, at the same time, I was going through the Ivey EMBA program and had a young child at home. It was very tiring and I was sleep-deprived most of the time. I had a lot of ambition, but with all the changes at work it didn't seem like I could use the knowledge I gained and there appeared to be little advancement opportunity. I felt trapped.

I remember my manager telling me: "What I worry about, Attila, is that you are making yourself miserable."

He saw that the root of my problem was me. Wow, it was all there about a decade ago, but I didn't get it. I didn't hear what he tried to get across. I thought it was the changes in the company, the reduced level of internal opportunities that was the problem and it had nothing to do with me. How wrong that thought was. Now I know. The great thing about finding out that I was causing my own misery was that I could fix it. One thing people don't realize is when they blame others for what is happening, they are giving away responsibility but they are also giving away their power to fix the problem. For me, it was as if a huge weight lifted off of my shoulders.

I was in charge. I had a choice. I decided what happened in my life. I needed to take ownership of everything that happened and will happen in my life in order to change and get back on a positive path of growth. Now, this is a sweet and sour type feeling. Regaining control is great, but can also be scary. Accepting that the pain and suffering was my own doing was a hard thing to do and it is something not everybody is ready to accept. It's so much easier to blame others than stand up and say, 'I caused it, I take full responsibility.'

Over the years, I have shared this information with many people and while most seem to have understood it intellectually, I know they didn't really internalize and understand its significance, just as I didn't when my boss at Meryl Lynch tried to explain it to me. For most people, it takes some sort of catalyst for the knowledge to become part of their daily life and in my case it was complete unhappiness. Looking at the external environment and finding faults or justifying our misery was so ingrained and easy.

The reality is that we always have a choice. We can't change or control the external environment, at least not by much, but we have full control over our thoughts and how we respond to whatever happens. We can choose how we want to think about anything at any point in time, even if it is something from the past. If I would ask you to think about the Eiffel Tower in Paris, France, I am sure your mind would see the picture of the Eiffel Tower, even if you have never been there. Then I tell you to think about the Eiffel Tower being five inches tall. Your mind makes it so, even if you know it's not really that size. Similarly, if I ask you to think about your car you can picture that. Now I tell you that your car was sideswiped in the parking lot. You envision that in your mind. You see how easy it is to change your thoughts?

We have the ability to do this all the time and we can create our own reality from our own thoughts. But in order to do this, we must be aware of our thoughts and we also must want to change. At this time in my life, I was ready to change and decided that instead of trying to change the external environment, I needed to focus on what was happening inside of me, what thoughts I chose and what decisions I made. It was liberating. The sun started to shine again, the clouds were blown away one by one, there was hope for the first time in a long time. I remembered how I used to be years ago when, despite the miserable surroundings I was in, like in the army or the refugee camp, or when I had nothing to eat, I still had my dreams.

I still held the sense of hope and was working toward a beautiful future. This is what I needed again – to stop looking backward and finding fault in everything. I needed to sit back in the driver's seat, hold onto my own steering wheel and view the world through a clean clear windshield again – focusing on the future.

What you are experiencing is only your life right now.

There is a better way and I will show you how to remember those long ago dreams and rekindle the fire you once had as you read the next chapters.

Why Not?

Chapter 3
The Competitive World

Why Not?

Chapter 3
The Competitive World

From a very early age, we learn to be competitive. Part of this is natural, but some of it comes from what we are taught. Watch how children play. They love to compete against each other. They run as fast as they can down the street just to get to the end faster than their friend. They ride their bicycles so fast their hair flies in the air. The joy and the happiness that comes from competing is intoxicating, especially because winning feels so good. It is our nature, in fact it is one of the laws of life, that everything grows and evolves into a higher existence.

This growth originates from our desire for more, better, or the newest version of whatever it is we want. As we challenge ourselves, we naturally compete against others and this competition is good for us. While in school, competition becomes even more ingrained. Children compete in so many ways and on so many levels. They compete for which class collects more for charity, which school wins the football championship or gets the trophy, who gets the highest mark, who gets the gold star and who is the most popular – the list goes on. Wanting more and challenging ourselves to achieve is so exciting and natural. This competition is also very innocent and pure as it is engaged in with the intention that the best competitor wins. It doesn't yet involve the various negative nuances we interject as adults. Although this youthful competition is always against another person or team, we rise to the top by bringing the best out of ourselves. We don't even think about lack and limitation. The only thing that we think holds us back from doing more or better is our own ability or drive to go for it and get it done.

Competition has so many good things about it, but it also has a downside. The winners are rewarded and celebrated while those who don't get a medal become the also-rans. Make no mistake, the rewards for coming out on the top are worth working for. Getting the best grades can mean entry into the best universities with full scholarships, getting jobs with the most prestigious institutions, getting in the newspaper or gaining fame and fortune in other ways. Everybody wants to be the winner, but there can only be one at the top in sports or in many other aspects of life.

We all know the saying "Life is like a horse race. The horse that comes in first gets the price that could be ten times more than the horse that comes in second. But the horse that came in first is not ten times better than the horse that came in second; perhaps only a nose length better." So winning certainly comes with rewards worth working for, it also gives the perception of a vast gap between competitors, even if the reality of that gap is quite small. Competing brings out the best in people, or at least in the largest part of them. Those who succeed in life and gain significant achievement are those who maintain their desire to get the most out of themselves. They challenge themselves to become better every day. They know that in order to get more out of life they need to put more into it. To put more into it, they need to become better in whatever they do so the service that they provide has a higher value, commanding a higher price in return. This desire to be better is effortless and natural. It requires no push from anyone or anything - it comes from inside when we are children.

I firmly believe this quality is in all of us, but we somehow lose it along the way as we encounter negative experiences. We lose our will to compete if we perceive ourselves to be unable to win. As children compete, most don't get the medals or the prize. Those who don't get on the podium often lose their desire to keep on trying and this is instilled a very young age for some. They rationalize why they didn't win. This usually is centered on others and the external circumstances and usually doesn't include anything about themselves. While many say, "Next time I will try harder," or "I will study more," these promises are not often followed up with real effort backing the commitment that was made.

Eventually, they feel worthless and unable to accomplish things. This is when it is the most damaging. None of us enjoy the emotion that comes with losing, so to protect ourselves from this discomfort it is easy to fall back to safety and avoid competing altogether. The protection from this bad feeling comes by not trying or not giving our best. So if we don't win, we can say 'I didn't really want it, I didn't want to win' or some other excuse, to put our minds at ease.

The reality is that losing sometimes, or occasional setbacks, are a perfectly natural part of life and the only time we become losers is when we stop trying.

Using babies as examples, let's think of the great accomplishment of learning how to walk. A baby will fall down countless times, but it doesn't seem to be bothered by it at all. A baby sees all the tall people walking around without their hands on the ground and that is all a baby is focused on. Falling down is just part of learning and there is nothing to it. A baby just wants to get up and try it again. I will never forget the moment each of my children managed to stand up by the couch and, holding on to it, took their first few steps.

The joy was indescribable. It was a marvellous achievement. Imagine the alternative. Picture a baby trying and trying and after falling down couple of times saying, 'You know what, this is just not for me, I didn't give my best, the carpet is uneven, my parents weren't teaching me right, my brother pushed me down, the cat scared me so I lost my balance. Now I give up.'

This, of course, is unthinkable. So why is it that so many of us settle for less than we want by giving up when we fall down a time or two? Pay attention to your own thoughts and the words of others around you and you will notice how many times people rationalize why they didn't win or achieve something. It's almost never about themselves. Notice how easily and quickly people tend to give up trying, usually after only one or two tries. I can't tell you how often I hear people tell me, "I am happy with what I have, all I want is happiness and peace of mind..." Of course everybody wants happiness and peace of mind. That is like a beauty queen saying she wants world peace. I have never met anyone who didn't want this or said, "I want to be unhappy and upset all the time."

Of course you want to be happy, but the question is, what gives us the conditions of happiness and peace of mind in the first place? People also say they are happy and content with what they have, but when they start talking, it doesn't take long before the list of reasons come out why they can't get more. There are always a lot of reasons (excuses). Everyone wants more, regardless of how much he or she has or achieved and whether we admit to it openly, the desire is still there. Wanting more is our nature and the law of life. Can it be that people say, "I am happy with what I have" to make themselves feel better and to give an illusion to others to make them think they are more successful; to make it look like they already reached their goal?

Make a Bigger Pie

The fact is that we can all earn our own medal. We all have unique abilities and talents and if we recognize and develop those gifts, they will allow us to achieve significant goals. These achievements will provide us with the happiness and the peace of mind along with the recognition of our peers and those we don't even know. I know what I am saying may not be the conventional way of thinking and living, but it is true. We all start out as children believing in limitless possibilities, but as we age we stop believing in ourselves and start believing that the world we live in is full of lack, limitations and hardship. But why is that? I'm sure by now that you know that I like to observe others when I have a question, and here is what I found. Everywhere I looked, there seemed to be bad news – one story after the other. It is so hard to escape the negative influences that we are bombarded with every day. Has this world gone mad? I wondered. We all know the cliché 'there's no news like bad news,' yet we pay attention to it. Even when we try not to, as I did, it is always right there in our faces. A few years ago, I got so fed up with watching the news that I simply stopped watching everything besides the business channels – and even they aren't completely immune to bad news. All other channels seem to require the wearing of a war helmet just to finish a half hour long program. The technical advancements we all enjoy add to our lives, but like everything else, there is another side to it.

We now live in an information age, meaning information is readily available to all of us at any time and news travels fast around the world. The media has taken full advantage of this new possibility of keeping people informed about every little detail, but have for some reason chosen to select stories that show suffering and hardship. This is because we have been conditioned to pay attention to negative news above the positive and they are in the business of ratings. It is so rare that some kind of a success story or significant achievement is shown that it becomes a rare treat.

People love to see the Oscars and the Grammys because we want to see people achieve, but we seldom see business or other non-entertainment type achievements, though there are many around, even in our local community. We must learn how to celebrate the positive instead of immersing ourselves in worry and fear. It never ceases to amaze me how events from across the continent impact our behaviour.

For example when there is a school shooting somewhere, let's say in California, all the news channels pick it up and it is on TV, in the papers and on all the news websites almost immediately and we all wonder if our children are okay. There is that little butterfly of worry that flutters in our abdomen—but why? Why do we let this impact us? Don't misunderstand, I am a loving father myself and know the value of the human life and the importance of providing children with a safe environment. But I am puzzled as to why news like this has to be in all the media, even across the continent 5,000, even 10,000 km away?

I am sorry for the people who were involved, and of course I wish these type of events didn't happen, but the reality is that I, like most people, have never been in that city, nor do we know anybody who was involved and I don't see why we need to know about it to start with because then we all worry more. If we take a closer look at what we are bombarded with every day, it is no wonder so many of us develop fear and anxiety about almost every nuance of life. It feeds the negativity that is alive and well in so many people, and it becomes the normal topic of conversation that there is something terrible going on somewhere.

The world is a big place with many countries, millions of cities and towns with literally billions of people, so finding something shocking is easy. Sensationalizing is alive and well and finding new ways of captivating people's attention is a science on its own. It takes a conscious effort to block out all these counterproductive influences, but it can be done.

The impact of all this negative conditioning is that we become very protective. We see the world as a dangerous place with only so much to go around. Because of this, we want to make sure we get our fair share, even if it is sometimes at the expense of others. Life is about growth and advancement, but often we set aside the internal growth and focus solely on getting more stuff. When we get something that is new and exciting, the newness eventually fades away, sometimes rather quickly. Like buying that brand new luxury car that we have been dreaming about, it makes us feel fantastic and worthy for a few weeks, but then it becomes the norm and so we need even more.

If we have the perspective that the world is a place full of lack and limitations, it impacts people in different ways. Some become reserved and shy. They develop a fear of losing what they already have and, in order to protect themselves, they make no effort toward advancement and stop trying to achieve more. They think trying something new is risky and risk can result in loss. What they don't realize is that, because life is about constant growth and advancement, those who stop growing automatically move backward. This falling back creates the result of losing that they so feared in the first place. So by not taking steps for advancement and trying to protect what they have, they automatically put what they tried so hard to protect at risk.

I have yet to find anyone who openly admitted they stopped growing and trying. Everyone likes to think they are 'growing,' though they don't actually do anything about achieving this increase in capabilities. All we need to do to measure our progress is to look at our bank book for last year to see how much we spent on self-development, how many non-fiction books we read, how many training sessions we attended that made us more capable and how much our living standard and income increased from the prior year. That will show us what reality is versus what we think it is. Viewing the world as full of lack and limitations makes some people very competitive with a strong focus on winning at any cost - even if it means violating the rights of others.

Competition in a world of abundance is a very good thing, but when competition takes place with a mindset of lack and limitation, it often results in steps that take things away from one person in order to benefit the other. Office politics are a very good example of this. I have seen individuals purposefully undermine the efforts of others in order to make themselves look better. Unfortunately, it is not a rare event. This creates a less than ideal working environment and frustrates every single person who is trying to achieve something, because all the members of the team are rowing different directions.

In times past, employees of corporations were considered assets and were treated as such. During these years, people and companies had longer term views and were working with one another. Times have changed, however. Downsizing became a common occurrence, beginning in earnest in the 1980's, as corporate mergers were rampant. This introduced fear and anxiety in people's minds, which has continued in the workplace even up to today. Managing financials from quarter to quarter became the practice, increasing volatility in spending and initiatives naturally resulting in the need to make the size of the employee base more agile as well.

One way to better manage the costs of labour was to change fixed expenses to variable by utilizing contract resources instead of full time employees. Then came the craze for outsourcing where companies were looking for any way they could to reduce their expense base by transferring functions and processes to other entities and countries where labour is cheaper. Technological advancements had a significant impact on efficiency gains as well and transformed the type of jobs that remained with companies. Those who had the drive to evolve continued to maintain their employment, while others weren't as fortunate. These are just some of the forces that transformed the relationship between employers and employees and created what is sometimes a very negative, competitive environment.

I remember that when I joined Merrill Lynch in the late '90's, the culture was wonderful. The company always wanted to hire the best and the brightest and allowed its employees to develop themselves over time and then achieve tremendous success. If anybody had a great idea, it was recognized and the company was eager to benefit from the intelligence and ingenuity of its employees. The focus was on creation and we all loved it. Then the early 2000's came along and a management change at the very top meant that there were now people in charge who believed people get in the ways of profit. Tremendous focus was paid to 'right sizing' and efficiency gains which translated to large layoffs. People were no longer considered the most important assets and the focus was on the costs that could be eliminated. Of course many of the best and brightest they had worked so hard to retain soon decided to entertain other opportunities. The change in the company's culture was incredible.

Many companies went through similar transformations, completely changing how employees feel about their existence in the workforce and their relationship to their employer.

Employers also saw their employees very differently. They were no longer assets, they were a liabilities. The sense of lack and limitations became well established. It's no wonder with this backdraft that people became protective of their territory and resorted to pushing their own agendas instead of focusing on what benefited the group with everyone working toward the same corporate objectives.

This constant struggle to get a bigger piece of the proverbial pie can be illustrated by imagining two ants in the forest fighting over a leaf, one pulling as hard as it can in one direction while the other pulls it in the opposite direction with all its might. They both are focused completely on advancing their own position and trying to make small gains over their opponent, not realizing they are in the forest with many more leaves all around them.

We don't have to think very hard to realize that all advancement in our history was the result of human creativity. We are all blessed with marvellous creative faculties and if we apply ourselves and focus on moving things forward, we can achieve anything we put our mind to. We are amazing beings and the question is not whether we are amazing or not, but how aware we are of that fact. We don't need to take anything away from anyone else; we don't need to try to make others look bad. We have within us everything we need to succeed. We just need to gain an understanding of all we are and learn how to apply ourselves. Then we can sit back and enjoy the ride. We have brilliance inside all of us ready to surface and we live in an incredible world full of abundance and possibilities.

Life can be and should be very exciting and I firmly believe that despite all the challenges we face, there is no other time in our history that is better to be alive than now. So many new things are invented every day and the rapid change we experience is the result of human genius and creativity we tend to take for granted. These are truly amazing and exciting times. We should all be joyful, happy and grateful for every day we get to experience.

As individuals, we have an opportunity to realize our potential in ways that was never before possible. Companies that will survive will be the ones that realize this incredible potential and capacity that exists in their organization. The companies that will take the management of their human capital seriously will prosper and achieve previously unseen heights, while the ones that continue to treat their employees as disposable commodities will vanish and soon be forgotten.

You can think of the abundance in this world like air. Even if every single person on the earth breathed in and held their breath, they would not use up all the air. There is a never ending supply and if we go about our work life and our home lives with that knowledge, we realize that there is no need for anyone to lose out to anyone else because there is always more. We need to stop trying to tug our leaf away from our fellow ants and realize that there is a forest of abundance all around us.

Creating this abundance in your own life is the next step!

Why Not?

Chapter 4
The Unlimited Potential
of YOU

Why Not?

Chapter 4

The Unlimited Potential of YOU

At the end of the previous chapter we talked about our infinite potential. It may be hard for you to believe this if you are being exposed to these ideas for the first time, but the reality is that we all have tremendous potential within. We were all blessed with incredible creative faculties and capabilities, which means we are capable of achievement that is only limited by our imagination. As you read this book, these statements may sound overly bold or perhaps too good to be true. You will soon see that what you read is fact and not fiction. In this chapter, you will learn about the infinite potential of your mind, how to use it properly and how it drives everything in your life. You will also understand how important it is to learn as much as you can about what you can do to further enhance your knowledge base. But first let's take a quick look at our history as the human race and how the way we live has changed over the centuries. This will help you understand the stage we are in and what you should be expecting going forward.

The human race has a very long history with many stages along the way and we could study our evolution for decades in great detail. I have no intention of doing that, but I do want to give you snippets of some of the stages to show you the progress we have made.

Ages ago, the ancient Egyptians had a very advanced civilization. Thousands of years prior to the birth of Jesus Christ, they were clearly brilliant architects and erected structures whose complexity still puzzles engineers today. Having said that, daily life was rather simple compared to today's standards. The primary modes of transportation, for example, were horse and donkey carts and carriages. People lived in simple houses, cooked over wood fires and cleaned clothes in the river Nile. If we fast forward the clock to Year 0 when Jesus Christ was born, we find that not much has changed from the times of the ancient Egyptians. The towns and cities people lived in had evolved somewhat and civil engineering has made them more liveable by producing roads and some rudimentary irrigation and sanitation. There are many other enhancements but they are all relatively minor. People still use horse and donkey carriages and still cook over wood fires and wash clothes in the river.

In the Middle Ages, though hundreds of years has passed, life is still relatively similar to the days Jesus walked the desert. Warfare and weaponry has evolved with many inventions; armour became more protective, but people still live in a largely agrarian society, growing their crops and raising animals to provide food and clothing. In many cultures, architecture and arts have made significant enhancements. For example, the churches, statutes and paintings being made during this time are remarkable and many survive even today for us to enjoy. The life of the average person however is still substantially the same as it has been thousands of years earlier. The main mode of transportation is still horse and donkey carriages, people still cook over wood fires and wash clothes in the rivers.

Now let's move forward a few hundred years again to the 1800's at the dawn of the Industrial Revolution. This is the period in human history when the rate of change in living standards and lifestyles dramatically increases at an exponential level. Steam-powered machinery is invented, manufacturing mass-produced products for the first time. It was the beginning of a brand new era where we rely less and less on our muscles to make a living and instead rely more on intellect. The rate of change from 1850 to 1900 far exceeds the change our species experienced in the previous 4,000 years. This is truly remarkable.

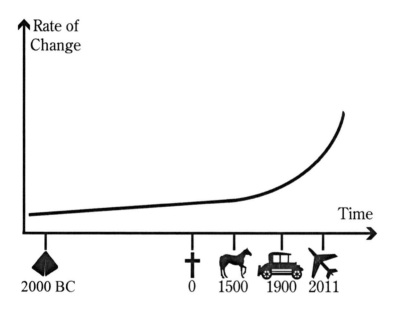

Despite the very slow and gradual growth that many of the ancients experienced in their standard of living, there were many who were thinking outside the proverbial box as far as personal development was concerned. As an example, we have the philosophers of ancient Greece, like Plato, who certainly provided a wealth of introspective knowledge and wisdom. There were very wise and learned men such as Nietzsche and Goethe whose works are still available today. Unfortunately, a great deal of invaluable work created by exceptional individuals was destroyed by those who feared the masses gaining knowledge. They recognized that knowledge is power and to maintain their own power, they needed to keep the masses in the dark.

We have all studied in our history classes about the book burnings by the Nazis during the Second World War. It is shameful that certain leaders of the past elevated their own interests above that of the people. What is also surprising is that the principles of living a successful life were discovered hundreds and even thousands of years ago, yet aren't taught in schools and aren't promoted to us by our leaders. I never really understood why and I still don't.

We know that the most important thing we can do for ourselves is self-actualization by striving toward achieving our fullest potential. As we reach this state, we all win. Not only does the person who achieved a higher state of awareness win, but everyone else does too since growth comes from achieving worthy goals and these worthy goals benefit us all. I would reason, then, that teaching the principles of living a fulfilling life is a subject that should be part of school curriculum. We would all be happier, healthier and wealthier if that was the case. But for now, it is important to know that educating yourself is your responsibility. You can read books and listen to knowledgeable people. Then you can discover what you want to internalize and incorporate into your life.

When we think about our evolution into the 20th century, we realize the explosive growth we have experienced. Even reflecting about the last few decades, the inventions that largely change the way we live are extraordinary. If I just think about the life my parents had versus the life I have compared to the life my children will have, it is mind boggling. When I was graduating from high school, I heard about the military and the space agency and I knew they used a machine called a computer, but never saw one. During my post-secondary education, I was trained on computers that used floppy disks and we learned DOS commands in order to do anything in these incredible machines. It wasn't all that long ago. Do you remember your first cell phone? It looked like a shoe box and was about as cumbersome – look how far we have come! I don't have to tell you; you know yourself that change is getting faster and faster. This trend will continue, and if we want to stay relevant, we must understand our minds a whole lot more and learn to use them significantly better. I think the biggest mistake we could make is to stop growing. When I start working with new clients or talk with people I know or meet with, I always ask them what they want to achieve. Far too often I hear 'I am happy with what I have.' When people say this, it concerns me. I tell them to think about the time the fax machine came out. It truly revolutionized the way we communicated with each other over distant lands and changed the work environment in any office.

Imagine if you told me then that you were happy with what you had – your new fax machine – and didn't think you needed to grow. How obsolete would you be by now? Life is constantly evolving and enhancing and if we want to maintain our lives and grow, we need everything we can to make forward progress. Those who choose not to grow make a decision to fall back. This decline may not be immediately observable, but over time it sure will deliver unwanted results.

Staying relevant, keeping up with the changes

If we want to advance, we will have to make a real, conscious effort to improve ourselves – just as I started to do the day I realized I was so unhappy. I had to make the effort, but knew that effort would need to be made in the midst of large environmental changes as well. Some statistics show that a large percentage of jobs that will exist in ten or fifteen years haven't even been invented yet. You know just as well as I do, those new jobs will not be in the labour sector. Now, some people may find this scary, but I find it exciting.

It is a popular myth that humans use less than 10% of our brains, but brain scans show otherwise. We do use our whole brains, but not necessarily for conscious thought and certainly not for their full potential. Much of our thoughts are in our subconscious, so we engage them as habits, all of which can be changed with focused and directed effort on our part. This is the type of personal growth I'm talking about. The kind where we look inside ourselves and make decisions about taking control of our lives and letting go of the habits that don't serve us. We all need to take this very seriously, but I don't want you to think that it will be difficult. Many of our habits and expectations actually cause our stress and make our lives hard. Life should be an absolute joy to live and it is so easy to make it so and you can create that reality. To do this, we need to make some adjustments to the way we think and a whole new world will open up.

To demonstrate how peoples' own thoughts create their life experience, I will give you an example. Let's imagine two people walking down Rodeo Drive in Los Angeles. One is full of excitement enjoying every moment of the experience: the famous stores, the celebrities around, the glamour and the wonderful weather. This person finds the experience magical. The next person walking down the same street at the very same time finds it too busy, too dirty, and thinks that seeing a well-known person driving by in a convertible Rolls Royce is upsetting because he shouldn't be able to live like that when his last movie wasn't even that good. This person dislikes being in the same environment as the other person who just loves what he or she experiences. Each person is making a choice and that determines their experience. This is a very simple example, but it illustrates the point.

What happens outside of us is neither good nor bad; it just is, and we make it either good or bad depending on how we think about it. Similarly, if we think about the rapid change in technology and life in general as a bad thing requiring us to do something we don't want to, life will be frustrating and unpleasant. Think about all the people who complain about upgrading their software or operating systems. If, on the other hand, we think about what a great era it is with all these new wonderful things that never existed before and look at things with the mindset of opportunities and the new inventions as marvels of human creativity, then our life becomes a pleasure to live.

You have to ask yourself, why not? Why shouldn't you choose to love life? We always have a choice. It is up to us. We can choose our own thoughts. Like 'change is good' for example. That is a choice. Most people would agree with this statement, but sometimes still find it very difficult to change their lives. The reason is that people resist change when they feel that they are asked or forced to change, but love change if it is their own choice. You can never make a change for anyone other than yourself, otherwise it won't last. It will be superficial at best. You have to want to change for you. By the time you finish reading this book you will already become a different, more aware person, who will want to change and will look forward to every day as a new venture. Your life will turn into a series of joyful events.

Though we live in an exciting era, we must be aware that we are all lifelong learners. Just being trained for a new job these days can take weeks or months, not hours as in the past. Life is complex and as humans evolve and advancements are created it takes more knowledge to make things happen. Our educational system is very good at providing people with facts and figures, but not particularly good at teaching people how to use all the information they learned. The art of thinking is not yet a subject that is standard in any curriculum, but I am sure the day will come when no one will be able to graduate without having an understanding of the mind and how to live a prosperous, healthy, happy and wealthy life. Until then, we need to read books like the one you are reading now to gather information that will show what to do to live a life with a constant feeling of pleasure.

By now you have a good understanding of why is it so important to focus on our mind and understand that all our power to change comes from within. Most people are conditioned to focus on the external environment and desperately try to change that those confines to fit their likes and needs. This is a losing battle, because although we can make small changes to our environment we can't control it. But we can control ourselves and by focusing on what takes place inside of us, we allow ourselves to see things differently, make better decisions and respond to events more appropriately.

We all grow up influenced by our surroundings and while this gives us a certain perspective, it isn't set in stone. Imagine a baby born into a Caucasian family in Toronto, Canada and the parents give the baby up for adoption. The baby is than adopted by a Chinese family. The child may grow up fluent in Cantonese or Mandarin, perfectly adapted to the local customs with no knowledge of the English language or the Canadian way of life.

Now let's imagine the same baby being adopted by a tribe somewhere in Africa. The baby would grow up perfectly suited to its environment by learning the language of the tribe and how to hunt with a bow and arrows. The child would know nothing about speaking English, Cantonese, and Mandarin nor would he know how to live life like a Canadian or a Chinese person would.

Let's now imagine the same baby gets adopted by a wealthy industrialist family in Zurich, Switzerland. The child would likely grow up speaking four languages, the three official languages of the Swiss plus English. The child would learn how to run companies, learn about the economy, how to behave in the Opera, travel around the world—the list goes on. You see how differently the child would see the world? You can see how different the child's value set would become simply from the influences the child had during his life, yet it would still be the same child and would have the exact same potential no matter where it was raised.

It is a proven fact that our environment and the influences we experience personally are more important that what we inherit genetically. We are all impacted by people who influenced our life during our upbringing and these influences determine the life we end up living. The conditioning we get will put limits on our thinking and we won't even realize that we all have the same infinite potential we were born with. We all have genius in us in some form, some unique ability that makes us one of a kind.

That talent could be and should be discovered, harvested and celebrated. Throughout the book I talk a lot about babies and children and I want to refer to them again. Children see the world as an abundant place with infinite possibilities and no limits. Their imagination runs wild and they believe that they can achieve whatever they want or dream about. Just because something they want and dream about doesn't exist yet means nothing to them. It just means whatever they dream about needs to be invented and created. To them it is an exciting opportunity and not a limitation.

The start of the paragraph is missing. Start it this way. – As we enter the education system things start to change rapidly. We are told the subjects we need to study, the questions we will be asked and how to answer them. As we move forward and become a part of the workforce, we work with the framework imposed on us in order to fit in and be accepted. We comply with the processes our company wants us to follow, the train schedule we need to mold our life to and so on. As life progresses, we get increasingly boxed in.

Over time, these limitations shift our attention away from those infinite possibilities and we believe in lack and limitations. But is it true? Do we live in a limited world? The answer is: No we don't. We just choose to think so. We believe that the limitations we see in our environment are real. But if this was true, how did all those wonderful inventions came about?

All things that have been created were just an idea in somebody's mind at one point in time. If we simply work within the perceived limitations at hand we only make small, incremental improvements at best. Yet, if we dare to dream we can achieve quantum leaps even if the masses think it is irrational to think that way. For example, Marconi was locked up in a mental institution when he declared that he would invent wireless communications. He dared to dream and believed in the possibility even though it wasn't something others did not think was possible. He forged ahead even though they thought he was crazy.

Think about the first horseless carriage, the first airplane, digital photography, 3D movies or iPads, to name a few marvellous inventions. The people who invented these marvellous advancements were no different and no better than you or I. We have the same abilities and potential. The only difference is they dared to dream big and applied their potential to a greater degree than most of us do. The beautiful fact is that we can all do the same. We all can achieve tremendous success if we choose to do so. We need to learn how and what it takes. Remember what I said about the baby growing up in various environments under various conditions? Whatever life the child ended up with as a result of who adopted the baby will make that particular environment with its own set of limitations the norm and the reality for the child. Think about your own life and question whether the limitations you see and believe in are real or the result of the common beliefs of the environment where you live.

Why Not?

Chapter 5

The Catalyst to Your Future

Why Not?

Chapter 5

The Catalyst to Your Future

By observing people, their ways of doing things and their ways of reacting to events, I can tell so much about an individual. I can discern how they feel, how calm or stressed they are, how aware they are and how happy they are with their life. It is a common courtesy to ask someone we just met how they are doing. While most people would give the standard answer 'good' I invariably reply "I love my life!" – and I do. You should see the reaction on people's faces when they hear this. My answer shocks them and brings initial disbelief. It is almost like they think I'm lying or trying to catch them off guard. They assume that nobody should love their life and that isn't the 'normal' response. Soon, they realize I am serious, and it is not just a blank statement, but my reality. Then they smile and say, "That is great." I agree and tell them that we should all feel like this, it is just unfortunate that so few people can honestly say that they love their life.

People know that there is a big difference between like and love. Getting to the stage of loving life really isn't all that difficult and I am convinced that as you read this book your happy meter will increase with each chapter by chapter. By the time you close this book, you will smile more and more because you know how beautiful life can be. You will think and feel very different about the possibilities in your own existence. You recall my own personal story from the first couple of chapters and you know that I wasn't always like this either—far from it.

I had my fair share of the dark years and, while they weren't pleasant, they helped me grow. Now those years are long gone. When I wake up in the morning, I am happy and look forward to another great day. For years, I was in the habit of saying various things off hand, but as I regained control of my life, I landed on my current saying that I love my life. In fact, for many years, I had the habit of starting my day by saying 'It is a great day to make money' and spent the rest of my day applying myself to doing exactly that—making as much money as I could. This may sound a little disturbing to you and you may be wondering how I could be so out of balance. But if you feel that way it is because you probably have a different interpretation of what money is than I do. I am a student and business partner of Bob Proctor, who always says, "money is the reward for services rendered." So when I say that I spend my day making as much money as I can, I am really saying that I am applying myself to my fullest to generate as much value and benefit as I can. This has worked for me very well for years. It really is the base for success in any discipline. Focusing on creating value and moving things forward makes us more valuable to our employers, business, or society in general and is what helps us gain happiness and peace of mind. As I studied the teachings of Bob Proctor and increased my awareness of who I am, how capable and perfectly made I am, I graduated to my current saying of "I Love My Life."

You are probably wondering how I made the transition from being in full-blown midlife crises to the joyful phase I am in now. I am now forty-five years old and know a lot of people in this age group. As I talk to people and we start chatting about life, I often hear people say that they are content with what they have, they don't want anything more. They think what they now have is their destiny. I know what they are really saying is that they do want more, they just haven't figured out how to get it and instead of looking for the answers they settle for what they have and call it good. In fact most people want a whole lot more than they need and settle for a whole lot less than they could get. But they don't need to settle for anything at all, and this is the best part. My way of looking at things is that I am about halfway through my life, I have never been more skilled and capable than now, why shouldn't I expect a significantly better second half? Why not? So I tell people, "Your Best Years are Yet to Come" and it's true. It is never too late to change your life and you aren't trapped into any type of life you might have right now.

I got to this stage by learning about myself and the truth about human potential. But still I wondered why some people are so successful while others struggle. I knew there was an answer to this question; I needed to find it. So I studied about my mind and what I learned made me feel like a treasure hunter discovering the mother lode, the shipwreck full of precious jewels and gold. I have always been curious, looking for answers to how life works. I read many of the religious writings and teachings of philosophers, but it is only recently that I discovered what I call the 'user's manual for life.' If I want to succeed, I need to focus on the inside. I need to understand what is happening in my own mind.

This is the key to the kingdom for anyone seeking a better life. If you study the lives and teachings of our leaders throughout recorded history, you will find that they had widely differing views on everything from the economy to business and perhaps disagreed on just about everything. But there was one thing they did agree on and that is 'You become what you think about'. Our life experience, our happiness, who we become and what we achieve all depend on our dominant thoughts. So we need to choose our thoughts very carefully. This is wonderful news for many reasons. Primarily because if there is one thing we can easily change it is our thoughts. The difficulty lies in becoming aware of our thoughts and making the ones we choose dominant. While most people believe they are thinking, they are really not choosing their thoughts with care. They confuse mental activity, random thoughts going through their heads, with thinking. That is really not thinking because there is no direction, no focus, no structure and no expected outcome. Simply 'things' flying across the screen of the mind is nothing more than noise. We need to learn how to choose and control the thoughts we keep in our mind. Most people live their life on autopilot.

Thinking is a conscious effort and we must make it so to focus on a specific subject, giving it our full and undivided attention with the aim of solving a specific issue with a specific goal in mind. As most of what we do on a daily basis becomes routine, we live our life on cruise control without actively thinking. For example, when we wake up in the morning and take a shower, brush our teeth, have breakfast, dress and go to work, it is all done without any conscious effort. In fact, sometimes you may not even recall what you did earlier. Even going to work becomes a routine after only a few days. I can't even guess how many times I ended up at the train station to realize I don't know how I got there. My mind had been on autopilot and my thoughts had been elsewhere. I have countless testimonies from people who drive to work taking the highway who experience the same phenomena. They have just enough awareness not to get into an accident and navigate their way through traffic, but the rest is pretty much a blur.

They don't even notice the buildings on the side of the road or anything else that is not related to their goal of getting to work safely. On top of that, many of our jobs are also based on routine. Most jobs require performing at least some of the same tasks every day. Running the same reports each morning, looking at the results, transferring the highlights/variances to another report and sending it over to another team is what a lot of people in an office environment do for a living. I did it myself for years. Going home at the same time with the same method of transportation, eating dinner at the same time every day, taking the kids to activities on the same night of the week at the same time is the routine of our days and thus our lives. You see how a lot of our life is a routine with no real thought required. The question then is, if most of what we do is routine and we do very little active thinking, how will we advance? Something must change. With these routine activities, we literally program ourselves the same way a computer is programmed. This programing creates a strong framework for us and when something happens we react to it based on what our conditioning demands. These reactions often aren't as effective as they could be or should be if we had more awareness of ourselves.

Instead of reacting, we would stop and think first, then respond. These responding processes will produce better results. I reacted to situations out of habit way too many times. Often, I regretted what I said or did. Not thinking and reacting on autopilot is not a good way of managing our lives. It is how hurtful words and phrases we heard as children become part of our vocabulary, even though we swore we would never say those words. It happens because we aren't thinking. Just like with computers, if we don't know how the programming works, then when something goes wrong, or we want to change the outcome, we don't know what, where and how to apply the necessary change. Similarly, if we want to improve our life, our position at work or our human interactions, we need to first understand our programing and how it got there in the first place. Armed with this knowledge, we can regain control of our destiny and achieve anything we desire. This is the first step toward living a successful fulfilling life.

The mind is the most marvellous creation in the world. With it we have the ability to become co-creators and create our destiny, the life we want and not the life we think we were dealt. As you read previously, we become what we think about and we have the ability to choose our own thoughts. It is also important to realize that we think in pictures. To demonstrate this fact, let's do a quick exercise. I would like to ask you to envision the Statue of Liberty in New York. I am sure it took no time at all to see it in your mind's eye.

Now think about your fridge at home. Think about how tall it is, how wide it is, how many doors it has, what color it is. By now you have a very clear picture of your fridge in your mind. With this little exercise I demonstrated two very important things.

• We do in fact think in pictures. Every thought we have has an associated picture with it in our mind. In our brain, we have cells of recognition that stores images of the experiences we had in our life. As thoughts come to our mind we activate these cells of recognition and that is how the images appear in our mind.

• We also realize how incredible easy it is to change our mind. You simply shifted your focus and attention to what I asked. You see how easy it is. You can use the same process when you have unproductive or negative thoughts flying through your mind. When you recognize them, you have a choice of either letting them keep you uptight, or you can simply change your mind to something more productive and pleasant.

Here is the million dollar question: If we do become what we think about and we do think in pictures, what does our mind actually look like and how does it work? Almost without exception everyone thinks that their mind is their brain. No doubt, the brain is an incredibly important part of our body and the brain does play a key part in the thinking process, but it is no more our mind than our pinkie finger. Mind is movement and the body is the manifestation of that movement. To clarify what the mind actually looks like, we need a visual representation. Without a visual representation we don't have clarity and confusion sets in.

Back in 1934, a chiropractor from San Antonio, Texas, Dr. Thurman Fleet, created what we now call the stick man. This representation of the mind is really simple, but I must ask you not to let the simplicity mislead you. Once you understand it, internalize it and use it to your benefit, it will allow you to change your life – reprogram your computer – into anything you desire.

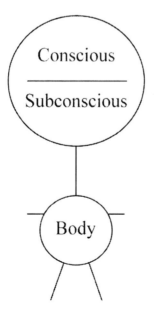

The large circle represents the mind and the small circle represents our body. The mind is much larger for a number of reasons, primarily, it is because it is so much more important than our body. In fact, it controls our body. The mind has two main components. The upper part is the conscious mind and the bottom part is the subconscious mind. The conscious mind is our thinking mind; this is where our free will lies. In our conscious mind we have the ability to accept, reject or neglect any idea and we can actively choose thoughts. The subconscious mind, on the other hand, has no ability to reject or neglect any ideas; it must accept everything it receives from the conscious mind. This means that the more we dwell on a thought, attitude or action, the more ingrained it becomes in our subconscious, like the drive to work. At one time we had to think about every twist and turn along the way – but soon we can do it without thinking and this is because it is now embedded in our subconscious.

The subconscious mind is where our programming lies. This is where our habits, paradigms, beliefs and internal map of reality lie. As our conscious mind sends information into the subconscious, then the subconscious creates our feelings and our feelings move our body into action. The action of the body produces the results we experience.

It is easy to identify what a person is thinking and what his or her dominant thoughts are – we can simply look at their results in life. That means you may tell me you are a positive person, but if I see a great deal of negativity in your life, then I know that you are actually dwelling on many negative thoughts. This is cause for excitement from my perspective because what it means is that the result you now see in your life are not a reflection of your abilities - it is simply a reflection of your thinking up until this time, which means it can change. It should also make you very excited because if you want better results in your life, you don't need to change the whole world, you just need to change the way you think. It doesn't matter what happened up until now, because your future has yet to be determined and it is totally up to you to decide what it will look like.

Once you have an awareness of your thinking, you can choose to gain control over it and determine what your dominant thoughts will be. The results will follow. This is a key step in the creative process and you can implement it right now. You can achieve anything you want once you understand these principles. Remember the subtitle of the book: Your best years are yet to come – and it can be true – it's up to you. It doesn't matter your age or stage of life, you can choose at any point to change your thoughts and enjoy a happier, more rewarding life.

The origin of the programming in our subconscious mind can be broken down into two main categories: hereditary and conditioning. Hereditary programming comes from the information we inherited from our ancestors through our genes, basically what we call instinct. We all have certain instincts that we are born with and one of these might be our flight or fight response when we are in a frightening or uncomfortable situation. We all have this hardwired into our mind, which is not to say we can't control it, but it is something we are all born with.

For the most part, our conditioning is the result of our experiences throughout the course of our lives, but especially from when we are children. At the time the baby is born the conscious mind is completely undeveloped and the subconscious is a clean slate. There are the instinctual actions like sucking or crying which we are born with and don't need to learn. Everything else beyond these basics is a learned behaviour. Simple things like eating with a spoon take quite a bit of practice and dedication but we soon master it. Riding a bicycle or learning to walk was the result of practice and a lot of falling down. Language skills, our habits, culture and beliefs were all learned as we were influenced by others in our lives, mostly authority figures. These authority figures include our parents, older siblings, teachers, religious leaders and other influential people.

This conditioning creates what I call the internal map of reality, or the programming in our subconscious mind. This is the framework or perspective we use to understand life's events and manage our everyday activities. We all completely believe this conditioning and the thought that our map may be wrong doesn't occur to us, like when I was in Hungary and visited places where people thought differently than I did. It never occurred to me that my programming might be wrong – I assumed everyone else's was wrong and that's what we all assume.

It is, however, possible that some or most of what we think is fact really isn't true. The fact is that there are no two internal maps that are identical. We each have our own reality and that is not absolute because there is no such thing. My parents were different than yours, my teachers were different than yours, my authority figures were different than yours, I grew up under different social circumstances than you did. These differences could be small or large, depending on our different influences. If you think about it, it's no wonder people disagree, because they translate whatever happened in their lives based on that relied-upon internal map of reality.

Cultures are larger blocks in our conditioning because a culture is a shared belief among a specific group of people. You don't need to think very hard or look for long to see that there are as many cultures as countries or even cities around the world. The way people live their lives in Toronto is based on a very different set of values, norms and habits than people in Budapest or Taipei. I think all of you can relate to this fact, especially if you had the opportunity to travel around the world or have relocated to another country. Companies, divisions within companies, or teams within the divisions, have their own specific culture. If you have ever changed jobs, you know what I mean – one may be open and creative, another oppressive and individualistic. We all want to fit in and to do so, we need to be aware of these differences and adapt to them.

No doubt having this map in place is important; we couldn't live without it. If we didn't have one we would be completely lost. This map tells us what the rules of the game are and we feel comfortable when we conform to some sort of beliefs and norms. Each nation, each religion, each group has their own version of how they should live. They all believe they are right. In truth, no one is 'right;' we are all simply different. We need to keep an open mind and recognize this. We also must accept the possibility that our way may not be the best and only way for a given situation.

Unless our life is a journey of constant joy and success, the chances are pretty high that some parts of our map will need to be revised along the way. How do we know if this is the case? If we find ourselves in the same predicament time and time again, if we keep getting the same negative results, it is a good signal that the problem may be with us. Think about this: If every job you had, you hated, maybe the problem is you. This is true of bad relationships too. At some point you have to realize that everyone else is getting better results and it's time to look inside for the answer. We just need to be honest with ourselves, acknowledge these reoccurring misfortunes and be brave enough to explore the possibility that perhaps it is we who need to make a change in our thinking, behaviour and actions.

People like me, who emigrated from another country, no doubt experienced this in a very profound way – it's what we call culture shock. You recall my own experience when I left Hungary and lived for a while in Austria. I didn't fit in at all in the beginning. The culture of the Austrian people was so very different from what I had known. Their way of thinking, doing things, humour and value set was very different than mine. It was a very difficult thing to experience such a mismatch, but I realized the only way that I would fit in was if I moulded myself to my environment. It simply wouldn't work if I waited around for the environment and all the people to conform to me.

I observed people and internalized their ways while gaining an awareness of my own. With some practice, I was able to control my reactions in many instances and when something happened, instead of reacting based on my Hungarian conditioning, I stopped, thought and responded. Needless to say, it made a big difference. One example would be my relationship to work. In Hungary, we had no incentive to work hard and do our very best every day. There was no such thing as unemployment. Everybody had a job. Positions were created in companies that provided no real benefit but they kept people employed. Naturally, people had no fear of not being able to make a living and had no incentive or drive to bring the best out of themselves.

When I went to Austria it became painfully obvious that if I wanted to eat, I had to produce. If I wanted to eat *well* I had to produce even more. People who worked had skills that provided real benefit and the more benefit they created, the more compensation they received. In Hungary at the time, manual labour was just as highly valued and compensated as intellectual labour. This was not at all the case in the West. Intellectual labour was much more highly valued. I realized pretty quickly that if I wanted to live better, then what I need to do was not to work harder but to work *smarter*. Instead of using my muscles, I needed to use my intellect. This is why education became so very important to me.

I had a similar experience of culture shock when I immigrated to Canada. The reality is that it takes years to become who we are and it can also take a long time to change, improve or evolve into a new improved version of ourselves. We have received our conditioning, or programming, over a long period of time with constant repetition and reinforcement. Reformatting our ways and thoughts isn't an overnight process, and takes just as much repetition and reinforcement. For example, while I became somewhat Westernized in Austria and learned a lot of very important life skills like the example I just gave, I still had a lot of Hungarian in me.

People in Canada thought my manners were odd and my jokes were not funny (and I thought I was a very funny guy!). It took years to readjust myself. I am quite certain many immigrants feel the same way and a lot of them never fully adjust to their new environment. One thing I realized relatively early was the impact of others on me. The influences of others have such a big impact on who we eventually become.

As you read earlier, associating with the right people is a key element in the kind of life we will eventually live. I realized that if I primarily associated with other recent emigrants, then the amount of time it took for me to integrate myself into the Canadian lifestyle would take a lot longer than if I spent most of my time with those who had either lived here for a long time or were born here. So I looked for ways to associate with Canadians who were more established and successful than I. I knew sooner or later their ways would rub off on me and I would become a different person.

From time to time, I saw people who felt more comfortable staying with their own kind and I'll admit that would have been easy. You don't have to feel awkward and you don't have to feel out of place. Time and time again their results showed little change and enhancement and that's not what I wanted for my life. I will agree that most people don't go through as significant a change as I did, but each one of us experiences changes in our own environment to some extent, if for no other reason than moving into a new neighbourhood, starting a new class or getting new job.

In every circumstance you can choose to enhance your life and change to be the best version of you. It's like the sales person who wants to become more successful so they hang around the most successful sales people in the office rather than those who barely survive. The same applies to a new job. Associating with those who are doing well will have an impact on us and it allows us to shorten our learning curve and go farther, faster. While we all know this principle, some people take it more seriously. Those who sit back don't realize they are costing themselves success. It is interesting that you often see parents move to certain neighbourhoods so their children can go to the right schools, make the right friends. If we do this to the benefit of our children, then we should consider doing the same for ourselves.

If we step back and take an objective look at ourselves and the people in our circle of influence we can see how much truth there is to everything I'm presenting. The way we think is the sole determining factor in whom we become and the kind of life we will have. I would reason then that if we want to do better in any area of life and live a happier, healthier and wealthier existence, we need to evolve. That means we need to become a more aware and more capable version of the self we are right now. If you are thinking well 'of course' I am glad you are getting it, but if we understand this truth, then why is that most people don't incorporate the knowledge or these beliefs in their everyday lives? They say one thing and yet still do something else.

The reason is that the old conditioning is so strong and so limiting that changing ourselves takes a real effort. Egos also come in to play. Some people absolutely refuse to accept the possibility that they may be wrong – even if it makes perfect sense. They won't accept the idea that they need to change on a deep level, even if they say they want to. We have all experienced a situation when we saw two people arguing over something and one was proven wrong but that person still would not accept the fact that they erred. This person usually comes up with all kinds of ridiculous counter arguments and perhaps even resorts to aggression rather than to simply say: "You know what? You are right, I was wrong." These may be some of the hardest words for someone to say and not only to someone else. It is very hard to look in the mirror and tell ourselves that we are wrong.

Emotional evolution is based on the basic premise that we have the willingness to modify our thinking and our interpretation of life. We know that our life is based on our conditioning, and we can agree that the conditioning is to a very large extent not even ours. It was put there by others before we developed our own ability to reason and accept or reject ideas or opinions we heard. All these people were well meaning I am sure, but what they gave us was based on the map they received from the people of authority in their life. We also know that we can grow and evolve. The conditioning we received is not permanent and can be changed to anything we want it to be. Granted, it takes an effort and an understanding of how to do it but it can most certainly be done. Now you have the awareness and understanding of how much power you have over your life experience. That includes what happens to you and the quality of life you live.

You can now see what I said earlier: that our environment and thinking are far more important than any hereditary conditioning we get. It is an absolute fact.

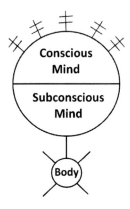

Once you grasp the basics of how the mind works, then we can focus on how it gets its information. We have our physical senses: we can see, hear, smell, taste and touch. These senses are like antennas collecting information from our external environment. Since we were born, we have relied on these senses to understand our world and collect information. In fact, if we didn't have these senses life would be a very difficult journey. Those who perhaps have one of these senses challenged can overcome what they are missing, but more than one of these senses not being available would make life very difficult indeed. That is why people like Helen Keller are such an inspiration. She was blind, deaf and mute, meaning she couldn't hear or see and thus she couldn't speak either. I am not even sure how one would ever overcome such a vast lack of senses, but it is possible. Having your senses intact not only makes life more pleasurable but also prevents us from harm in many ways. For example, if we weren't able to feel hot or cold, how would we know when something is burning us or if our toes were getting frostbitten? We wouldn't feel the pain and whatever caused the pain could destroy our flesh.

The challenge is that most people spend their entire lives relying on these five senses alone and they aren't aware of all that they really miss. This is a problem for three reasons. First, our senses take in an incredibly large amount of data every moment and we don't process or use all that information. We don't have the mental capacity to dwell on every detail. Though we store all the information, we are consciously aware of only a fraction of it. We literally filter out all the information that doesn't fit our dominant thoughts. Like the person driving to work on the highway doesn't even notice the buildings on the side of the road, or a person standing in a packed subway car filters out most conversations and other noise.

Our minds must have some sort of ranking system to determine what is important and what isn't and so it filters the information based on our dominant thoughts. For example, have you ever gone to a car lot and bought a new car – maybe you picked a green one – because it wasn't a model or color you saw much on the road and you wanted something unique.

The minute you drove it off the lot, it seemed as if cars of that exact model and color were everywhere. It's not that they weren't there before, but because you didn't have a similar car, your mind filtered out that little bit of information as unimportant. Once you had the new car, your thoughts focused on it and so your mind reordered the information and you were shocked.

The reason this is important is that we are filtering out information every day that could turn our lives around. It is amazing how when we decide to do something, everything necessary for its attainment shows up. What we needed was always there, we just didn't 'see' it because it was not relevant to our goals at the moment.

The second problem with relying totally on our senses is that they can mislead us. You all know about optical illusions and magic tricks, like when we see a ship going out to the sea it seems as if it sinks further out in the horizon or when we see a person disappear on stage. We know that these events are not really happening the way our senses tell us they are. Think about the railway tracks that seem to touch each other in the distance. We know that is not true either. Our senses can trick us into believing something that isn't true or allow us to make assumptions that aren't correct, not to mention all the things our senses are unable to detect which pass us by. We know there are sounds we can't hear, like a dog whistle. We know there are particles like neutrinos or bacteria that we can't see. We can't see the radio waves or certain light emissions, but that doesn't mean they don't exist.

The last problem with the senses is that if you consider your physical body with all its parts and organs including the five physical senses, you realize that you can find all these in a pig or a monkey or in many of our other friends from the animal kingdom. So the big question is: what are the factors that make us human? It is these factors that you must understand in order to become all you were intended to be.

Chapter 6

Your higher self

Why Not?

Chapter 6

Your higher self

Our emotions and our ability to think on an introspective level, and even change who we are, is what makes us human. A monkey is a monkey and will always behave as a monkey, but humans behave in all different manners and have the ability to change this at any time. In this chapter I will include an in-depth analysis of the intellectual faculties. These are the factors that we control and manipulate to create our own realities. I will show how they work, what they do and how can they be utilized in the work place or in the everyday life.

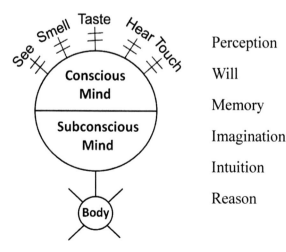

Perception

Will

Memory

Imagination

Intuition

Reason

Our intellectual faculties are part of our conscious mind. Here is where we think and can originate, neglect, accept or reject thoughts. Surprisingly, almost nobody can recite what these intellectual faculties are and how to properly use them – and those few who can don't necessarily understand how to exercise them. In fact, you can even think of them as mental muscles. They can and should be developed and, if they aren't, they will atrophy from disuse.

Once you gain good knowledge of the faculties and incorporate them into your life, you will no longer react when something happens, you will instead Stop, Think and Respond. These are the faculties that determine the level of awareness we have, which is the key driver for the quality of life experience we enjoy. Here are the faculties with a brief description of each.

Perception – is our point of view. I am sure you have seen countless examples of when something happened and the people who observed the event each had a completely different translation or recollection of it. People in the police force see it all the time when they investigate a crime scene. Witnesses may give them different versions of the truth and it's not because they are lying. It is because each person has their own filtering system, so their minds picked out different things that they thought were important and ignored the rest. Now, if I were to hold up my book with the front cover facing you and the back facing me. I could tell you that there is only text on the cover and you would tell me that is not true. The picture of a yacht is on the cover. We of course would both be right but the reason we had a different perception is because we observed the book from a different *perspective*. The description of the book is on the back cover so I was telling the truth as I saw it and so were you. This is a simple example, but you need to understand that using this faculty in any human interaction is very important.

At times, perhaps in an office setting, people aren't willing to hear others' views and opinions. However, sometimes the voices or views we don't react the most strongly to are the ones that can be the best ideas. We have all heard a million times to 'think outside the box' but all too often the thoughts generated outside the box are discounted because they don't fit with the 'rules' that we have inside the box, which is our perception of how things should be. So it is very important to keep an open mind and listen. Don't immediately assume that something won't work, can't exist or is not possible just because it doesn't fit with our current understanding. In fact, most all technological innovation and advancement was the result of something coming into existence that people previously thought would not be possible like space travel, wireless communications, 3D TV and many other great advances. It is almost never a good thing to become set in your ways or entrenched in a particular thought process. Accept the possibility that there may be another way of thinking about a certain situation and give this alternative view a fair shot. Even if we rule it out after careful analysis, that alternative perspective may spark additional new ideas taking us closer to the solution we seek.

I find traveling is a very good way of enhancing and even challenging our perception. By visiting different cultures and nations we observe different ways of thinking and doing things. Being exposed to these alternative methods opens our understanding of what it is to be human and enriches our lives in many different ways. I firmly believe that Canada is arguably one of the best places in the world to live. It didn't happen by accident. There were many contributing factors to create this highly advanced society and it is still an ongoing evolution, as are all nations.

One of the factors that I believe enhances the experience in Canada is that it is a truly multi-cultural country. If you have an opportunity, come and visit Toronto or one of our other larger cities and you will see this for yourself. You will find an incredible array of nationalities where ever you go. People who come to Canada from other countries come mostly for a better life and they are all willing to work to achieve this dream. Each nation, and each group of people, bring numerous unique qualities with them that, when combined with the unique and effective qualities brought by other nationalities, make a highly effective and progressive mix. Their knowledge and best practices are shared as everyone works together and what used to be unique to one group becomes the norm for everybody else too. This has made a massive difference in the way Canada grows.

It goes without saying that being exposed to many different cultures on any given day naturally creates an acceptance of the many alternative ways people think. Canadians are very open-minded and the willingness to entertain and accept other ideas contributes significantly to our way of life and the high living standards we enjoy.

There are societies, on the other hand, that keep to themselves and aren't keen to integrate people from other cultures, different races or who have different ways of doing things in general. These societies may find it difficult to adjust to the evolving world and the many changes impacting their lives. This reinforces the idea of how the environment influences who we become and how perception makes a difference in our behaviours and the decisions we make.

Keep an open mind and accept the possibility that the way you look at things may not be the best way. Realize that not only there is no shame in admitting that there is a better way, but we should celebrate the discovery of that better way. Thank the person who let you see an opportunity to become more than what you are right now. Eliminate the fear of what will happen, what people will say or think if you decide to change one of your beliefs with a higher thought process. You will know that 'I evolved, I now have a higher understanding, I am now more capable.' Focus on the positive aspect of growth and what it can bring you. Everyone likes a winner and when you improve, you become a winner for yourself. You don't compete with anyone else. People respect and appreciate the person who has the security and the confidence to admit they are wrong and want to do things in a better way.

As we already discussed, in the corporate world change is constant. Often management and company direction changes, and with that comes a change in priorities, procedures and perhaps values. These changes are necessary so the company can evolve with the marketplace. Senior management recognizes the forces impacting customers of their enterprise and sets the new course. This new direction filters down the management chain and ultimately reaches the rank and file. This is where the rubber hits the road, as they say. The effectiveness of the new strategy is highly dependent on the manager's ability to understand their employees' perceptions and paradigms and enable them to make the changes necessary. From an employee's perspective, the new strategy may be the latest and greatest in the line of many and they may think that it, like all the others, will soon pass as well. Some employees will explain to their friends and co-workers all the reasons why the new strategy won't work and instead of working on delivering what is asked of them, they slow the progress down. They don't do it with bad intentions necessarily, they do it because of their perspective on how the company has operated and because of their lack of clarity on what the leadership wants to achieve.

Managers need to be very aware of this problem and the underlying reasons for it. They must be skilled in understanding the prevailing perceptions and consider the emotions and motivations of their employees in order to properly manage them. By understanding the power of the intellectual faculties, managers in any organization can more effectively create and manage change while retaining and developing the best employees.

Will – gives us the ability to focus and stay the course. You know the saying: "when the going gets tough, the tough get going." Whatever goal we set for ourselves, whether personal or corporate, we will encounter challenges along the way, guaranteed. To succeed we must remember to focus on the end destination, make the necessary adjustments and keep moving forward.

If we look at the world of sports, we see incredible examples of people with very strong will. To become the world champion in any sport takes years of dedication and practice every day. People do this even though it may seem totally illogical when you think of it from a mathematical perspective. The odds of them getting to compete in the world championships are miniscule, and the odds of winning even more remote, yet they must work each day and believe that they will be the one that wins. For example, a sprinter preparing for a 100 meter dash at the Olympics spends many years of training for hours every day without fail.

When the race begins, the competition is over within ten seconds, but it takes years of dedication to get to that level of competition. I am sure there were countless times when that athlete didn't feel like waking up early in the morning and going down the track, but they also knew that without this dedication they would never participate in the Olympic competition and would never have a chance to win the medal they desired – even if that chance was remote. If they didn't work every day, it wouldn't happen.

The corporate world works the same way. People who succeed more than others don't give up at the first sight of difficulty. They know that challenges are part of the course and are nothing more than an opportunity to display their strength and dedication. Although I have achieved success in my own career, I know there is a lot more to me than I have been able to display thus far. One of the reasons I have not achieved more is that I changed direction too easily. But that is okay. I recognize that I chose that path and now I can choose another. The past is the past and I can't change it, but the future is still ahead of me and the opportunities are limitless. The choice is mine on how to go from here.

The only limit I have is the limit I now put on myself. I am halfway through my life and know that my best years are yet to come. Your best years are yet to come as well, as long as you don't give up and settle. Continue to set big goals and keep on working toward them. Use your will to achieve your dreams by focusing and moving forward each day. The thrill you will get from accomplishing each step on your own path to success will fuel your motivation to accomplish even more. Will gives us the ability to focus. It acts like a magnifying glass.

I am sure when you were a child you also harnessed the sun's energy to start a fire on a piece of paper or pile of dry grass. If the magnifying glass was out of focus it wasn't very effective, but if we carefully found the right angle where all the energy from the sun ended up in a small focused point, the impact was nothing short of amazing. Our mind works the same way. When we focus our attention, our effectiveness escalates exponentially and we can achieve anything we want. We astound ourselves as to what we are capable of accomplishing. If, on the other hand, we linger and lurk around life without applying ourselves in a resolute manner, the results - or lack thereof - in our life will reflect that.

Using the will is the foundation of effective thinking. In a previous chapter I mentioned that thinking is a very hard thing to do. It requires undivided and fixed attention on a specific subject seeking answers to a particular desired outcome. It requires the blocking out of all the 'noise'" thoughts that keep on popping up in our minds with subjects often unrelated to what we are trying to think about. Some people call it 'scattered brain,' describing the inability to focus on a single thing. If you are not sure what I am referring to, pay attention to your thoughts and see how many diverse ideas pop into your head.

For some reason, people focus a lot better at work than in their private lives. My own team tends to be able to block out the rest of the world, and apply their undivided attention to the task at hand. This is a great quality and very good news for a manager. People or employees who do this are a lot more effective, productive and make fewer mistakes than those who are all over the place and can't seem to keep a single thought in their mind for any period of time. I am not sure whether those that master their ability to focus at work practice their ability in their private lives and with the same intensity. I think everyone should, but most probably don't. We all tend to relax and coast when we get off work and that's normal. But focusing on what you want to accomplish outside the work environment is just as important, and up to you.

Memory – gives us the ability to remember and recall events. Some people say they have terrible memory, which of course is not true. We all have perfect memory. All the information we ever received through our sensory factors or thoughts that occurred to us are all stored in our mind. If you feel you don't have perfect memory it is because you haven't learned how to recall the data. From time to time something triggers thoughts in my mind and events or situations come back to me from various stages in my life, even from my very early years that I hadn't really thought about or recalled until that very moment.

I can still vividly see the bedroom I shared with my brother as a child in the small mining town in Ajka, Hungary. I remember the houses, the people, my toys, my friends. In fact, I pretty much remember everything about it. It was nearly forty years ago. I am also amazed when I talk to my parents and my father who is now in his eighties still recites verbatim poems he learned in elementary school. He also recalls details of his experiences during World War II when he was only a teenager. He remembers the bombings and how a Russian soldier hit him on his chest with his machine gun and threatened to kill him if he didn't give the soldier his pocket watch and all the food they had in the house. He even recites the words the solder yelled at him in Russian.

As I meditate, I often reflect on my life and re-live events in my past. It doesn't take a lot of practice to recall long forgotten events and be able to recall clearly what happened even decades ago. Give it a try and you will be amazed how good your memory really is. As I mentioned earlier, we think in pictures and we have neurons of recognition where we store those memories. We can easily recall these visual representations and with that comes the associated words, the smells and the feelings. There are many good books available about strengthening your memory and I would encourage you to practice your recall.

Using memory effectively in the work place is very important. Leaders tend to have very good knowledge of the businesses they run and can recall large volumes of detailed information about it with ease. This is an important quality in leadership, especially in quantitative fields where having that knowledge stored can help in decision making. Our memories also help us in making personal connections with people we recently met, or met in passing. Everyone likes it when you remember their name and this is something that you can improve with practice.

You are a culmination of your past experiences and being able to recall these experiences when you are reviewing the root cause of some of your behaviours is essential. We often wonder why we act the way we do and the answer usually lies in our past somewhere. Being able to locate those events then gives us the ability to analyze them and change those behaviours that don't suit us.

Imagination – is what allows us to be creative and to visualize the possibilities even for things that don't yet exist. Without imagination we wouldn't have anything new created—*ever*. Everything invented by humans was once just an imaginative thought in someone's mind. This book was just an image in my mind for some time and now it is a reality. The computer that I am typing on was just an image at one point as was the chair you are sitting on as you read the book. Executives in companies who are developing new products or a new business strategies, entrepreneurs opening up new markets or creating new segments of existing markets are also using their imaginations. People in the world of sports often visualize winning. The subconscious has no ability to tell a real image from an imagined one, so as they envision the steps they need to take to win, their body responds as if they are practicing. Many very high level athletes know and believe that the mental part of their game is just as, if not more, important than the physical part.

I'm sure you have heard famous leaders, whether business or otherwise, called Visionaries. The interviewer asks them: What do you see in the future? How do you see the market next year? And other questions that always center on future events and circumstances. All these Visionaries know how to imagine a future state and because they know that thoughts are things, so they are not afraid to imagine. They believe in the possibility of the image they hold in their minds becoming a reality and they spend all their energy and potential in taking the actions to make that image a reality. This is how we move forward. Those that don't imagine/visualize a future state stagnate. They don't drive change. They may *allow* change from time to time if they are asked to do things differently, but they themselves don't create the change.

Those who are very successful look at the possibilities with an open mind and even if what they imagine/visualize doesn't seem possible at the moment, they don't hold back from going for their vision. We all need to use this very same method to drive our own destiny, whether in our professional or private lives. We need to exercise the ability to imagine what we want and then focus on achieving it. We have an idea of ourselves and this determines the kind of life we live and who we become. This vision is powerful and we can never outperform our image of ourselves. If we want to live a 'larger' life, we need to develop an image of our 'larger' self and keep this new image constantly in mind.

I find it interesting to talk to people who call themselves 'realists.' They purport to believe that they live in the moment and only believe what they can see. The problem with this perspective is that it robs them of their future. If you only believe what you can see and only focus on the moment, then you will only ever get the exact same results you have now. How can you ever achieve more if you refuse to imagine a different life for yourself?

The whole basis of achievement is based on being able to imagine a different and improved existence. It is what spurred explorers to discover the New World. They first imagined that it existed and then set upon a way to get there. I'm sure when they first set out across that vast expanse of ocean there were many detractors who kept telling them they would fall off the edge of the earth, but they believed. That is the kind of imagination you must have - the kind that you can hold onto and believe in with all your heart. It's that belief that will get you there.

Intuition – gives us the ability to pick up energy from others. By energy, I don't mean the electrical kind from a wall socket. I mean the kind that helps us make a connection with someone or know that an individual we just met is loving or hateful. I'm sure you have all at one time or another walked into a crowded room of people you didn't know – maybe at a party or other type of gathering. As you look at people and shake hands, you get an instant impression of the kind of person you are meeting with. That is their energy. You might notice that often very outgoing people marry very introverted spouses. This is because we intuitively seek balance in our relationships.

Some people also say that if prayer is the way we talk to God, intuition is the way God talks to us. It is that feeling you get when you know a decision or action is right, even though you really don't know why. We use this intuition all the time in our lives, but when we learn to use and trust this faculty, we can take our life up a notch. For example, if you are a sales person, intuition is essential in order to gage what energy the client is in. Feeling the mental state of the prospect allows the sales person to modify the conversation in a way that the client would be most conducive to receiving it. Not having the ability to assess the client on an intuitive level can make the meeting very short and unproductive. Intuition is how we pick up the mental state of others. We know when those around us are emotionally hurt, sad, happy or even angry without having to say anything. I can walk into a room and know immediately if my spouse is unhappy (hopefully not at me, but that's another story!). These signals give us the opportunity to meet the other person where they are mentally and even help bring about a more positive perspective.

I remember attending some company meetings where, although nobody actually said anything, the tension in the air was so thick I could have cut it with a proverbial knife. You all know what I am talking about. There were then other meetings where everybody felt great, wanted to be there and the energy in the room was easy going and fantastic. It is well-known that we are all just a mass of energy and depending on our mental state, we radiate this energy (or vibrations) to those around us.

Our own mental state has a direct impact on people around us. Individuals, especially in a managerial or authoritative position, need to be aware of this. Their mental state has a direct impact on their teams and organization, even if the boss is trying to hide it or never says anything. Those around him or her will pick it up. However, when the boss is always calm and collected, the teams are happy and productive. I know this from personal experience as a people manager.

There were times when I was unaware of the impact of my own emotional state on my team and didn't understand the implications. I was not aware of how to control my own thoughts and when the going got tough, I radiated bad or negative energy. Even though I tried not to say anything, my team felt it. In more recent years, as I gained the knowledge and the awareness of how intuition works, I worked hard to create a very positive mental state at all times. I know for a fact that this has impacted people on my team and people I work with in great and productive ways. This is a perfect illustration of how if we want to have better circumstances what we need to change is not our external world, but what happens in our own mind. We all have the ability to affect everyone around us and we do so each day either positively or negative whether we are trying to or not. We have the ability to choose the positive; we just need to do it.

Reason – gives us the ability to process the innumerable variables in our world and make sense of things. This is the highest function we have. As you recall, in our conscious or intellectual mind we have the ability to originate, accept, reject or neglect ideas. We make those choices with our reasoning faculty. There are professions that specialize in this one aspect of our thought process – like lawyers or negotiators, to name two. Both of these professions also require the effective usage of other faculties, but reasoning is certainly a critical one. Reasoning relies on our frame of reference, as well as our conditioning or paradigms. A lawyer would rely on the laws of the land to guide him or her during trials, but in order to effectively argue a point before a jury or panel of judges, they must be able to frame the argument and/or evidence in a way that helps the listeners draw a reasonable conclusion as to the facts of the case.

Reasoning is very closely tied to our ability to make decisions. If there is a single quality that has the biggest impact on an individual's life or an entity's existence it is the ability to make effective and timely decisions. People who succeed have great decision-making abilities while those who struggle to make effective and timely decisions find their lives to be much harder. In our everyday life we make decisions countless times each day. Most of these decisions are small in their significance and, in fact, are made without any conscious effort. When we operate in a routine mode, most of the decisions we make are on auto-pilot as well. Bigger decisions like buying a new home or a car require consideration and conscious deliberation.

When we think about our new home, we consider the area, the distance to schools and other infrastructure, the condition of the house and of course, the price. We carefully weigh all these variables and by using our reasoning of the pros and cons, we eventually buy the house we want to make our home.

Then there are even bigger decisions we need to make from time to time, decisions that can have a significant impact on our lives, such as who we marry, or decisions on the direction of the company or group that provides our livelihood. These big, potentially life-altering decisions sometimes create a lot of anxiety and difficulty for some, while others see through the issues and make a decision with ease. Why are some people so good at making decisions while others find it so difficult? The answer again goes back into the way we think and the frame of reference we have.

Those that have a clear and well-defined goal can ask themselves how this issue relates to what they want to achieve. If it has no relation at all then the idea can simply be rejected. If it is relevant, the next question is whether the outcome is something that we want or not. If not, then the issue can be neglected. If we do want the outcome, we need to determine if this event will move us closer or further away from our goals. If it moves us closer to the goal than the last thing, we need to consider is whether doing this will violate the rights of others or our core values. Having a framework like this available makes the decision-making process much easier. It also requires having a clear and well-defined goal.

There are many people who struggle with decisions to the point they are almost paralyzed in fear because they are so afraid of making a wrong decision. This is not a problem with their ability to reason or their intelligence level. They have a self-confidence problem. They are so unsure of themselves that they don't trust their own ability to reason through a problem and choose the right path for themselves. They allow the 'what-ifs' to cloud that decision-making process and as soon as they make a decision they regret it because they fear it was wrong. For many of these people, this can stem from a perfectionist mindset and I see a lot of this in the corporate world. The facts and data are analyzed to death and by the time a decision is made it's so far down the road as to be almost inconsequential.

The ability to use and develop all your faculties requires that you understand yourself and believe in your own abilities. Then once you learn to exercise your mental faculties your ability to know what you want and why is enhanced. I've been around people who were very in tune to their mental faculties and often could make decisions in minutes that many have taken someone else days or weeks. I have even experienced this myself and I know that the time it takes to make a decision has nothing to do with the weight of the decision. Instead, it speaks to the fact that their faculties are well-honed and they completely trust the information they are gathering by utilizing them.

You naturally have all these faculties available to you as we were all born with them. We each need to develop them and use them to our benefit and the benefit of others. If you find yourself thinking that you can't, realize that it is nothing more than the limiting thoughts I have been talking about. Every time you catch yourself thinking these negative thoughts, stop and mentally set them aside. Now ask yourself 'How can I?' The more you eliminate the limiting thoughts and get in the habit of looking for the ways to get something done, the more you will see opportunities to help you achieve whatever you want. The answers are there; you need to ask the right questions and open your mind to receive the answers. As you focus and practice, these goals will become your dominant thoughts and the help and assistance you need to reach those goals will appear. Your dominant thoughts will determine your life, the experiences you will have, and the person you will become. With this process you can and will reprogram the conditioning in your subconscious mind, one day and one thought at the time.

Recognize your dreams and desires; don't suppress them, celebrate them. Desires are nothing more than unexpressed possibilities. You can achieve anything you want; I know this from my own personal experience, not from some theory. I have lived it and you can too.

You also must understand that no amount of reading or memorizing this information will make the difference. It is the understanding and the application of this knowledge that will give you the new outcome you are looking for, so it requires action on your part. You can start the process today by exercising your imagination. Start dreaming again like when you were a child, because dreams are the start of determining what your goals will be. They are not some fantasy or unrealistic notion. Thoughts are things and dreams have created many an empire.

As you keep an open mind and accept that you will do things differently than you did before, you will notice how much better your life will become, how much more fun you will have and what a wonderful and marvellous world we live in. One of the things I noticed was how much I laughed. It's not really something I thought about much, but there used to be days that would go by without a smile or laugh. Life is too short not to enjoy every day and now not one goes by that I don't laugh or smile at something. Dreaming allows you to reignite your passion for life and start really living rather than just existing.

Seven Steps to Happiness

1. Learn to dream again and have full confidence and faith that you have the ability to achieve them.

2. Embrace the thoughts and desires that come to your mind as you dream and don't worry about the 'how.'

3. Once you realize what dream you want to focus on, start exploring the possibilities of how to achieve those big, exciting dreams. Know that finding ways that won't work will take you closer to finding the ways that do.

4. Utilize your will to power through problems when difficulties arise and it seems that what you dreamed about is not possible or too hard. Remember the saying: When the going gets tough the tough get going.

5. As you work through the various twists, turns and obstacles, listen to the intuitive knowing in your head that shows you the way and ignore the thoughts that rationalize or tear down your confidence.

6. Don't be discouraged; know that any situation can be looked at from different perspectives. Keep an open mind and explore the alternatives. Sooner or later you will find the way, even if the direction you need to take is not apparent from the start.

7. Enjoy the peace and calm that comes into your life as you are living completely on purpose and working toward your new life.

Chapter 7
Captain of YOU

Why Not?

Chapter 7

Captain of YOU

By now, you see that our life experience is uniquely ours and it was created from our thoughts followed by our actions. We have everything that it takes to do anything we set our minds to. We never need to settle or accept the circumstances as they are.

Everything we experience in our lives is a reflection of our thoughts up until this point in time and not a reflection of our abilities or potential. If we want a better, more fulfilling existence we need to raise our awareness about our capabilities and seek to understand the governing laws of the universe. These laws are very precise and are applicable uniformly to all of us, whether we know about them or not or whether we accept their validity or not.

In order to move forward, it is important to understand and accept that we've created everything in our lives and we must take full responsibility for it. We have made countless decisions that created the circumstances we experience, be they good or bad. We always had a choice in every circumstance, whether we knew it or not. While we can't control events, we can control our reactions to them and whether we allow those circumstances to taint our perspective or not. This may seem a bit hard to believe and accept, but if you really think about it, you will see how true it is.

Personal responsibility is the foundation for creating a future that is positive. Once we internalize and accept that we are in charge, and we have always been in charge, it gives us a kind of sweet and sour feeling. It is sour because we realize that we could have done better. Perhaps we have done things in our past that we are not particularly proud of or wish we had done differently. It is always easy to be smart and make all the right choices after the fact. It is our nature to do our best given our level of awareness and knowledge at the time. Hence those past decisions that we now are second guessing or regretting were made with the best of intentions at that point.

One thing for certain is that the past is in the past and we can't change what has happened. We can and should learn from what transpired but should leave the negative emotions associated with it behind us. Some people hold on to past experiences and can't seem to, or want to, let it go. They carry the burden for their whole life. This guilt or anger is very destructive. It impacts our physiology, creates stress and anxiety and is instrumental in developing all kinds of illnesses. When the mind is not at ease it creates *dis*-ease. Scientists have studied the impact of the mental well-being on our physical body and there are many documented findings showing the direct link between the two.

Not letting go of the past also creates an intellectual burden that we carry and it impacts every decision we make. Like all the programming we have in our mind that got ingrained by constant repetition, this guilt and anger we build by constantly remembering and reliving the events becomes who we are. It acts as a filter in our subconscious mind, a key part of our internal map of reality, and will impact our decisions almost as if we are still trying to alter the past outcome. That, of course, is simply not possible.

Guilt and anger can become limiting beliefs that have no place in our future. Accepting these limiting beliefs as reality is quite common in our society. Most people I talk to have them and very few actually realize how paralyzing they are or see the need to eliminate them. One of the accepted norms is to hold a grudge against someone based on past events and use that to discredit them. Politicians are especially known for this. How often do you see a leader's past called into question by the media as they talk about events that happened decades before? They intimate that those past events would prevent this individual from doing a great job in their current or future assignment. What if all the decisions you made in your twenties were presented to those you want to work for today?

This is a good example of when we can use our reasoning faculty and decide whether we let news like this influence our decisions or choose to ignore it all together. We don't need to live in the past and we don't need to hold grudges against others or ourselves. It serves no purpose. We need to forgive and allow the past to remain where it belongs. It's time to move on. What happened has already happened and can't be changed. Let's focus on the direction we are heading. I am sure you still remember the driving analogy I gave in an earlier chapter where the windshield became a rearview mirror because it was focused on the past. Forgiving everything in our past will make a significant change in reducing the size of that rear view mirror in our lives and allow us once again to look forward to our future.

The sweet part of the acceptance of full responsibility for our lives is that we feel in control of our destiny once again. Having control is liberating. It is a powerful feeling to know that we can influence our future, the outcomes of our efforts and can achieve the goals we set out for ourselves. We aren't seeds blown around by the winds of life but co-creators who decided what the future has in store for us. I am a firm believer that the main reason people experience a mid-life crisis or feel unhappy is due to the perceived lack of control. It's when the external circumstances take charge and we become reactionary. The antidote is to regain control, which starts with taking ownership and responsibility.

I talked briefly about forgiveness, but it is an essential part of calming your mind and releasing the past. There are additional methods we can use as well. Meditation has been proven to be very effective in not only improving mental abilities by harmonizing the right and the left hemispheres of our brain but to also aid the healing process, slow aging and inhibit the development of illnesses. I myself am an avid meditator as are my wife and oldest child, and many in my group of extended family and friends. We have all experienced tremendous benefits from this tool.

Meditation allows you to reconnect with yourself and remember your goals. You can focus your mind and rid yourself of any negative influences that accumulate each day. This gives a feeling of peace and serenity and allows you to start the day in a positive mindset. It also allows you to overcome some trying times by reducing worry and stress.

My mom, who is in her seventies, developed cancer last year and it was very difficult news both for her and for all others in our family. She is a fantastic person but has spent most of her adult life worrying. In fact I believe she would worry if she didn't have something to worry about! I know she is not alone and that many people live their lives this same way. It seems that there was always some bad news that she needed to think and talk about. I firmly believe that this constant worry, compounded over many years, has changed her body chemistry and given the cancer cells an environment in which they could flourish and develop.

Once she received the diagnosis, my mom became open to alternatives on many fronts. She was willing to hear how negativity impacts her and was eager to read books about positive thinking and self-development. She also started to meditate and wow, what a transformation she went through! In addition to the usual medical interventions like surgery and chemotherapy she was also given very good nutritional supplements. I believe it was the combination of helping her mind and also giving her body the vitamins and minerals it needed that has helped her stay cancer free.

She is now a brand new person with an abundance of energy, a positive outlook on life and an overarching feeling of calmness and joy. While for decades she was influenced by external events, she now knows that she is in charge of her life and she finds it very liberating. You can do the same and you don't have to wait for some devastating diagnosis. You can start right now. Instead of fighting a losing battle against the external world we can't control, we can simply focus on our internal which we have complete control over. At that point, everything changes for the better.

Once you regain control and are truly in charge of your life, it is time to seek the direction you want to head. Goals move us forward and give a sense of purpose. Goals, in fact, are very common and many of us set them all the time. In order to differentiate the insignificant goals from the ones that really matter, we can put them in three generic categories. The first category are what I call the everyday goals – your 'to do' list. These might include stopping by the mall after work or buying a new piece of furniture. They are things that need to get done in the normal course of life and are easily achievable. Although these little goals provide some short term direction, there is no inspiration in them, no excitement and no challenge. Achieving them is not even a second thought and you don't question if they are possible you just do them. Once they are achieved, they are largely forgotten and more small goals take their place. There is no long term direction in these small everyday goals; they are just a task list. At work they might include clearing out your email inbox, or compiling monthly reports – again not big goals just more 'things that need doing.' These are the 'A' type goals.

The next category of goals ('B' type) are the ones that require some planning and are longer term and more complex in nature. You might want to take the family on a big vacation next summer. That requires research, financial planning and scheduling for everyone in the household. Or you might be considering moving to another town, which would require relocating your family and finding a new job and housing. At work, most companies plan their year in advance and usually have a three to five year high level objective they want to achieve. They look at their product offerings, market trends, economic forecast and financials. With careful consideration they plan to gain small improvements across the board, generating acceptable returns for their shareholders. Most of these plans seem reasonable and achievable. Having a high degree of predictability built in provides safety. What it doesn't have is inspiration and this is true on the personal front as well. A great vacation is nice, but once it's over, it's over so there isn't that inspirational quality to these mid-range plans.

The third category of goals ('C' type) is the one that both excites and scares the living daylights out of us. These are the very far reaching, stretching-type goals. These goals are based on dreams, not on our perceived reality of what is possible or what we think we can get. These are the kind of dreams that assume we have no limitations in what we want to achieve. They are the real source of inspiration and provide us with fulfillment and the drive to succeed. These goals get us excited, get us out of bed in the morning and make us look forward to another day of achieving them step-by-step. The real essence of a great goal is that it makes us grow as a person. If the goal does not include growth, it simply is not the highest level goal.

For example, buying a new TV requires no growth at all and therefore should be on our 'task' list rather than set as a true goal. On the other hand, if we allow ourselves to acknowledge our dreams and set goals based on those ideas, we will grow – we will have to in order to meet the goal. The more growth a goal requires, the better the goal. If we already know how to achieve the goal and it requires nothing more than us just doing it, it limits our growth.

The best goals are exciting because they are so big and scary. We don't know how we will achieve them when we set the goal, but the excitement of possibility keeps us going. The fact is that most of the fun in achieving the goal is figuring out how to accomplish it. The journey is so much more important than the moment of accomplishment. As the saying goes: the real benefit in achieving the goal is not what we get from it as a result but who we become in the process.

From time to time we even see this in the corporate world when companies achieve incredible growth and earn our admiration. The way they achieved it was by dreaming big. Not looking at the limitations or to achieve small incremental gains but reaching farther than anyone ever thought possible before. They dreamed big and inspired members of the management team and all the employees. They know that the most important asset they have are their employees. They are aware of the unlimited potential each employee has and they are willing to harness this available human capital.

Employees of companies like this are much happier, more productive and achieve so much more. I firmly believe that at this stage of our existence, companies that will prosper are the ones that make a conscious effort to understand the human mind and the human potential. I find it rather interesting that companies work so hard to get a five or ten percent efficiency gain by streamlining operations and tinkering with processes while paying no or limited attention to improvements in their employees' effectiveness by utilizing the power of their minds.

Every company I have worked for has prided itself in hiring the best and the brightest. In reality, once the employee was on board, little attention was given to bringing out their highest potential. Sure, we all have to take continuing education courses all the time - in my case, banking related in regards to money laundering and compliance - but I have yet to find a course that helped me think better or showed how to increase my effectiveness by changing my thoughts. For people to be truly effective in the workforce, they need three things: inspiration, awareness of their capabilities and support from their management.

Understanding and capitalizing on the limitless capabilities of the human mind is the new frontier. Quantum leaps are possible in every area for those that use their minds and the achievements can be astonishing. The society and world that we live in today was the result of human ingenuity and it was not a fluke. Mankind has tremendous promise and only a very small part of that has been tapped thus far. Management teams need to understand this, learn about getting the best out of their people, and allow them to shine.

Achieving these big goals makes us more capable and moves us onto a higher plane because we understand how much power and ability we really have. Things that previously seemed impossible become possible and we realize that the only thing that held us back from achieving our big goals was our lack of awareness and belief. Awareness is something we gain along the way by looking for the solutions to the challenges we face on our journey. It may be small at first, but as your awareness grows, so does your confidence.

We must accept that we don't need to know every step necessary to accomplish our goal prior to the start of our journey. We just need to be very clear about our destination and the first few steps we need to take. The rest we can figure out along the way. This 'figuring out' of things and processes we weren't aware of, provides us with new knowledge and makes us more capable. This is a very important source of happiness and fulfillment.

It is confusing when I hear people say they don't want more or that and they are happy and content with what they have. They say that all they want is peace of mind and happiness. I am puzzled because I know that they can never really achieve those things without constant growth. Peace of mind and happiness are conditions that are the result of getting the sense of achievement and the knowledge we gain by realizing how capable we really are. The more we practice improving ourselves, the more peaceful and happy we become because we are gaining confidence in ourselves and fulfillment from our actions.

Everything we need is already inside us. We only need to become aware of it by discovering talents we didn't know we had, achieving things we've only dreamed about, and feeling more comfortable with who we are as an individual. Internalizing the knowledge that we can achieve anything is a great emotional high and gives us faith in our ability to move forward. Faith is another key concept in achieving our goals, because without it we will not achieve much. Faith is the ability to step out into the unknown and trust that the path will appear. It is knowing that you will reach your goal even though you have absolutely no idea how it will happen. Those that either don't have faith or have faith that is not firm will always see the glass half empty and pride themselves on being a realist. What they are really doing is focusing on the negative and limiting their potential. These limits are self imposed and have nothing to do with their true potential. So dare to dream and know that any dream you have is a possibility seeking expression. If you can dream it, you can achieve it.

When working toward your goals, it is important to think back to the intellectual faculties – especially to the faculty of will. Any big goal will require determination and persistence and a well-developed sense of will can help you stay the course. Set your goal as a long-term exciting vision, keeping a constant eye on it and take effective actions every single day to start making your way to that goal. Some take longer, some are shorter, but one day those dream goals will come true. Of course, you will be challenged along the way. There will be situations that move you off course, but that is okay because it is part of normal course and how we learn. You can think of focusing on your goals much like when an airplane takes off and the pilots activate the autopilot to fly the airplane to a very specific destination. The exact coordinates of the target destination are the goal and the computer with the autopilot program will make all the necessary corrections along the way to reach the desired destination. The airplane will never fly in a straight line from point A to point B. Wind conditions, weather fronts or other factors will move it off course frequently, but the autopilot will make the necessary corrections and ultimately get the airplane to the desired destination. Achieving your life goals works the same way. Once you set it, after careful consideration, don't change the destination just because something happened or you encountered a problem. Simply change the course, make the necessary adjustments along the way and keep working toward achieving your goal. Changing the destination will not get you where you want to go and will frustrate your efforts. To illustrate this point, I will give you an example:

Living in Toronto, Canada gives us the opportunity to vacation in the southern US on a regular basis. We spend most of our vacations in Florida in one of the buildings owned by the time share company I belong to. Each time we go, we first decide where we want to go and when we want to go. We make a reservation and start thinking about the itinerary and the activities we want to engage in. We usually have a fairly good understanding of what we would like to do because we have been to similar areas frequently. Let's say if we go to Daytona Beach, we will allocate some time to enjoy the beach, go deep sea fishing, miniature golfing, and perhaps drive over to Orlando for shopping or to go into the Team Parks. We know when we are going to leave from our home and when we are coming back. So we effectively set the course because we know where we are heading.

Every time we go, we drive. It is a long journey and the distance between my house and our building in Daytona Beach is about 2,000 km. Along the way, we may experience road closures, accidents or be required to take an alternative route for some unknown reason. When these challenges come up we never change the final destination, we make the necessary correction and drive on a different highway but ultimately end up at the planned destination.

Now imagine, if due to extreme snow conditions in Virginia, instead of avoiding the mountains and going by a different route we decided to cancel the trip all together and agree to just think about a new trip next year. It sounds a little silly because we all can see how to easily avoid or go around the problem, but most people live their lives with this sort of 'give up' or defeatist attitude. They have no clear understanding or commitment to the final destination and every time something happens, instead of modifying the approach, they cancel the trip altogether and select a new, easier destination. Without committed decisions and persistence in staying with the goal through thick or thin, the destination is never reached.

Using the same trip as an example let me illustrate what can happen if we have no committed end goals in mind at all. Let's suppose our family is comfortably seated in the van and we are leaving our home for spring break in Daytona Beach, Florida. We leave early in the morning and by the afternoon everyone gets tired of the long trip somewhere in Virginia. We all think about the fact that we still need to drive another twelve hours. It seems too long to us, so we decide that instead of continuing our journey, we will just drive over to Virginia Beach instead. We adjust the course and arrive by evening. We spend the night in the hotel and anxiously wait for the morning to see the ocean and go swimming in it. The morning is glorious, the sun is shining and we are all full of excitement. We go down to the beach and find the water is very, very cold. Not being able to swim in the ocean takes a lot away from the experience, so we decide to pack up and go a little further south. We decide to visit Hilton Head in South Carolina – maybe that will be better.

After a long drive, we arrive at Hilton Head and the scenery is breathtaking. It is as beautiful as it gets. We are excited again and can't wait to find a hotel to stay at. We drive around from hotel to hotel but everything is fully booked. We know it's late in the day and that probably by the next day some people will leave and free up some rooms for us. So we drive away from the beach and stay in a hotel just for the night.

The next morning, we drive back to the ocean front and try our search again, but with the same results. We discover that people vacation here not by the night, but they book at least a full week and to make a reservation its best to start the process at least a year in advance.

Well, it is unfortunate, but we decide to stay a bit longer and enjoy the beach. The water is still pretty cold and the parking is very expensive, since we have to drive from our far away hotel to the beach. But we try to make the best of it and decide to give it another day. The next day things aren't much better, so we decide to get on the road again. We head to Daytona after all. We arrive and to our surprise it is bike week! The town is full of thousands of rowdy Harley Davidson riders. There is a great deal of noise and partying going on everywhere - it is just not the place we want our children to be. So by the next day we decide to drive over to Panama Beach. It's about a day long ride but hey, it's better than being around all those bikers right? We end up in Panama Beach and the beach is beautiful. The water is deep blue and clear and the sand is like soft powder. It is fantastic, but wait a minute - it is Saturday already! A full week has passed by since we left, and now our vacation is over and we have to start driving back home.

None of us would want to vacation this way, but many people live their lives this way, with no real commitment for what the end goal is, constantly changing direction and never really enjoying the journey. They alsways think something is always wrong, and years go by as they try and try but nothing really good comes out of their efforts and they are left feeling frustrated and disappointed. It is at that point many start to settle in and accept that this is the way life is. They say, this is enough for me; this is my destiny; I don't want more; all I want is peace of mind and happiness. The sad part is that they don't have to settle, this is not their destiny, but it is what they are choosing to accept. The good news is that they can choose to 'un-accept' it at any time and really live the kind of life they have thought impossible up until now.

Fear is alive and well in most of us and it will rear its ugly head on occasion. Some people are so fearful that they are almost paralyzed and unable to do anything effectively or try anything new. Making decisions becomes very hard because of the fear that the decision may be wrong. This is especially true with big decisions like setting those big and exciting life goals. Many people wonder how they can determine what those goals should be when they don't have a crystal ball. The answer is that they must allow themselves to dream and then recognize the reoccurring dreams as the ones they really want. This is a simple process but requires dedication and an open mind.

At an early age we had a lot of dreams and we didn't limit ourselves. As we grew, we all boxed in the dreams that we no longer considered a possibility and much of this was due to outside influences that told us to be 'realistic' and quit 'dreaming.' Most people give up on their early dreams and sometimes get to the stage when their dreams are limited to winning the state lottery because life to them has become a game of chance and not something they can control. But once we recognize that we have infinite potential and can achieve anything we want, the dreams appear again. If we then look for the signs of what really makes us happy, excited and fulfilled the answer to our questions clarifies.

It is a good idea to carry a little notebook around with you at all times and when we get those sudden inspirations and cosmic messages, write them down. Soon there will be a clear pattern and our purpose in life will reveal itself. When we find our purpose and we start to realize it, success comes our way with a speed that can shock us. When we live our lives according to other peoples' expectations and do things that perhaps our parents or friends think we should do, we don't have the same level of joy as we do when we live our own dreams. We simply aren't interested or driven enough to be able to differentiate ourselves or stand out.

When we are 'on purpose' it takes almost no effort to succeed. It feels that way because it is something that we want very much. We don't need to force ourselves to do anything because we are doing what we really want to do. We want to excel and be the best we can be because it is attached to this big dream in which we are emotionally invested. Finding our purpose in life is the first step to making dreams, and I mean big dreams, happen. In this mode, we are not stressed but calm and excited because we see endless possibilities. In short, you feel like a kid in a candy store. Life becomes good, fascinating and full of hope and possibilities. Being 'on purpose' is the ultimate high.

Living with purpose doesn't have to be a full time existence right off the bat, although it is much better that way. There are those that are unwilling to take the necessary risk in going for their dreams as soon as they discover these truths, and who like the safety of the steady pay check. That's okay, too. They can still do this in their own time and as they gain strength and confidence they can make the changes necessary in the timeframe that works for them. There is no reason why someone can't have a dance studio in the basement, or teach classes in the evening or volunteer in the senior's home making a difference in people's lives while still holding down a job that pays the bills. When people take part in these extra activities, even on a small scale, that are in alignment with their purpose, they find that their stress level goes down, their happiness goes up and their effectiveness and joy in their regular day job also improves. It is a win-win situation.

When I explain the steps involved in living your dreams, people all too often say something like "I would do it - but I don't have the time." We are all busy and we all have the same twenty-four hours in each day. It is not a question of busyness, but one of priorities. I like to show the following chart to people to drive the message home:

There are seven days in a week each with twenty-four hours creating one hundred sixty-eight hours available per week. This is what we have to work with – everyone gets the same amount, no one is cheated or receives less and no one can have more.

Most people work forty hours per week and commute about two hours per day going to and from work. Let's assume that is about fifty hours we no longer have available to put our plans in motion.

Most people like to sleep eight hours per day and there are seven days a week, so that is a total of fifty-six hours that are also no longer available.

We all need to shop, take the kids to activities, exercise, or do other activities let's say for another thirty-two hours per week (four and a half hours per day). So let's do a quick tally:

Available hours	168
Time spent working	(50)
Time spent sleeping	(56)
Time spent with life	(32)

Available time remaining: 30

Your numbers may vary from this somewhat, but the basics will remain the same. Guess what? We have thirty hours available. It may not feel like you have that kind of time, but when you think of the time you spend watching TV, on the computer, or chatting on the phone, you really do have a few hours every day that could be devoted to something you really want. Even if we just utilize half of that available thirty hours, it won't take long at all before we see a significant change in our results. Fifteen hours per week amounts to seven hundred eighty hours a year, which is almost twenty forty-hour weeks. That is like working full time for five months. That is significant and means that if we used all thirty hours, instead of just fifteen, it would be like working fulltime for ten months – almost a full working year!

We like to convince ourselves that we are too busy, but really we aren't and just because we have a jam-packed schedule doesn't mean that all the things on that schedule are moving you forward. There are usually an easy ten percent of activities we engage in that we can simply stop doing. It can be something as simple as shopping once per week instead of everyday, or getting together a carpool to so you only have to take your kids to school one day per week. The bottom line is that in order to make change, you must make it a priority and not believe the lie that you are too busy. No one is ever too busy to live a better, happier life.

I hope you are as excited about this as I am. You can see how utilizing this time with meaningful and effective activities would change our lives for the better and in a big way. Wouldn't it? You have the time, you are gaining the knowledge, and your best years are yet to come. Why not? It's up to you and you alone.

Why Not?

Chapter 8

The Secrets to Ultimate Achievement

Why Not?

Chapter 8

The Secrets to Ultimate Achievement

We all have unique gifts and abilities and they are always seeking expression. From time to time, we receive impulses for something that resonates with us, something that captures our imagination and soul. Perhaps we hear someone talking about what they do, or see some activity that feels like a perfect fit for us and we know this is what we should be doing too. We must embrace these impulses and recognize their patterns and what they are telling us. Becoming aware of these impulses is all about listening to that intuitive faculty and, if we listen, it will help us identify our purpose. For some, finding this purpose takes time and effort, but it is important not to rush it and wait for your specific purpose to reveal itself and then you can move toward it.

I realized that I plateaued in my own career. I had achieved some level of success, but wasn't able to move on to more senior roles, even though I tried. For a while, I blamed the external circumstances for my lack of forward motion, but after studying the principles that I've shared with you, I concluded that the real reason was I was not living 'on purpose.' I observed those who managed to get to the top and into the most senior positions in our organization. That's when I realized they all lived and breathed their work. I don't mean that they were workaholics, although some did work very long hours, but that they did what they enjoyed doing so it didn't even seem like work to them. Their work was effortless; they didn't wake up in the morning just to get a pay check, but were instead genuinely interested in what they did and wanted to become better in their respective roles.

This was the missing link in my life. I didn't have that innate love for what I did. Intelligence and hard work can take you many places, but to succeed requires the role to match that person's true purpose.

As I said, for some, finding their purpose comes easily, while for others it requires more effort. I was onc that took more effort and I struggled for a while. I was searching for information, inspiration and guidance for finding my own purpose, but even with that, quite a few months went by before I found my calling. The reason it took a while was because as I searched for my destiny, I was still looking at everything with my old limiting mindset. I was viewing things from my old perspective, not fully understanding that things can be looked at differently and that my way was just one of those possibilities. I was also very good at using my reasoning faculty to convince myself why I was never going to achieve the idea that kept coming to my mind as my purpose.

Working with human potential and helping people realize how capable they are was almost a foreign concept in every job I previously held. But my intuition kept telling me this is the area on which I should be focusing on. Eventually, it was so obvious that this is my purpose, I couldn't push it back anymore. Instead of telling myself why I couldn't do it, I looked for ways I could. This was a turning point. Since this subject interests me more than anything else, it was easy to immerse myself in my studies related to personal development.

Soon, I enrolled into Bob Proctor's Life Success Consultant training program, his coaching program, his Thinking Into Results program and I also studied the teachings of many other life teachers. I soaked everything up like a sponge. My life has turned around so quickly and so drastically that I was amazed at the difference. Instead of being tired most of the time I had an abundance of energy, the sun seemed to shine brighter and I was once again optimistic about the future. Being 'on purpose' is like nothing else, as it gives you such a positive and exciting perspective on your life. My daily life was now infused with anticipation and a sense of accomplishment. The more I allowed myself to explore this new destiny, the better my life became. Every day since has been filled with joy. Every day has made a difference. I now love my life.

Setting big, exciting, and scary goals becomes easy if we know who we are and what we want to do. Life takes on a different and higher meaning for us. Instead of being the proverbial hamster on a wheel, we regain control, learn to look ahead again and are inspired each and every single day to be the best we can be. As Maslow identified, the highest level of existence we can achieve is self-actualization. He was so very right, but so few people actually attain it.

It is important to understand how this idea affects the corporate setting as well. To get the organization to perform at peak capacity, it requires the employees to be inspired and dedicated to achieving big, meaningful goals. When the senior leadership creates the company strategy they take a great many factors into consideration and set the goals for the organization based on what they think is reasonable and perhaps even what they think is a stretch goal. Leaders that are very effective are the ones that can excite and inspire their organization and work with their team to understand this goal and progressively moving toward it. To be able to understand how people think and how to motivate them, allows the organization to move forward faster and farther than their competition. It also has the additional bonus of creating a happy, joyful workplace which, in turn, allows that company to attract the best minds available. Goals work best when they are clear and well understood and while this is true personally, it is also true in the workplace.

Every organization, every team and every person should have a concise, written goal. This goal should be well thought out and static over a longer period of time as this allows for growth toward the goal. Individuals and organizations may think that by frequently changing their goals they are nimble. What they really are doing is reacting to changes in the external environment instead of delivering their vision and creating that glorious future state they envisioned from within. As the saying goes "The best way to predict the future is by creating it."

Carrying around goals in your head isn't enough. Writing down the goal is a must because this gives it more validity in your own mind. Reviewing it often helps internalize the vision, the target state. Writing goals down regularly (by hand) accelerates this internalization process because it involves all the senses. Simply keeping it in mind, or typing it, does not have the same impact. Writing causes thinking; thinking causes feelings; feelings cause the actions and the actions produce the results. Since I learned this truth, and practiced it by writing my goals down every day, I was able to achieve my goals much faster than when I didn't write them. Give it a try and you will see the impact for yourself. One positive quality that will come from this process is the development of persistence. The bigger the goal we set out to achieve, the more resistance we will encounter. Nothing significant gets ever achieved without going through many, and sometimes large, hurdles along the way. It takes courage and dedication to stay with something that at times seems too difficult or appears to have way too many obstacles along the way. But by staying the course and focusing on the end goal, we will always find a way to break down the barriers or discover an alternative way to get to the other side so we can continue the journey.

The principles I am describing in this book can be viewed as common sense and perhaps many people would even say 'I know that' but here again, few people live their life this way. You may 'know' it in your head and it is logical, but the question is whether you practice it in your life. Take a moment and reflect. Think about whether you have your purpose in life identified, if you have a big exciting goal that you have written down, and if you think about this goal all the time and take effective action every day to achieve it. I would suggest that you also ask your family members, friends and associates to find out whether they do or not. Most likely they will say that they do have goals, but if you ask about what kind of goals and if they have them written down, you will likely find they really don't and, if they do, they only have 'A' type goals and they aren't written down. That means that there is a really big gap between what people know and say versus what they do. Another consideration is that if no one can tell by the results in your life that you are working toward something, than you aren't effectively working toward your goal.

Be mindful if you take my recommendation in finding your purpose and develop a big, scary 'C' type goal, those around you may not be traveling in the same direction as you. Be careful who you ask for advice and who you listen to, because sometimes those around us can be detrimental to achieving our goal. It will be very easy to be influenced by those who belong to the majority, who aren't in control of their lives and have not demonstrated their ability to shape their destiny in a meaningful way. Receiving advice from people like that, especially if they are close to us, can take us off our course and allow us to fall back into our old ways. You must practice your will to stay the course. Don't let any influence or any circumstance take your eye off of the wonderful image you have in your mind. Don't let anything throw you back into the old ways of going with the flow, and reacting instead of creating.

I recall once hearing: life is nothing but a series of problems and our success in life depends on our ability to solve these problems. So there is no sense being bothered by difficulties or complaining about them because they are actually benefitting you by contributing to your long term growth. Look forward to new challenges, as each one brings you that much closer to your dream. Many people are in the habit of complaining, but like any other habit, it can be changed. Use your will and remove those non-productive and limiting thoughts. Instead, focus on solutions and what you can do to overcome the obstacle. If you address any problem with questions starting with "how can I?" you will find the solution each and every time. The answer may not come right away, especially at the beginning, but if you will persist it will come. All you need to do is seek and you will find. As it says in the Bible: ask and you shall receive.

Dedication and full faith in your abilities will aid you significantly. These are qualities that every successful person has. When coupled with the internal drive of making every day count, you will know you are on the right path. Life is nothing more than a series of days and those who have successful and fulfilling lives are the ones who have more successful days than unsuccessful ones. Life is always a percentage game, but as you learn your purpose and start living in positive anticipation of your dreams, your percentages skyrocket. Start everyday with the vision of your goal and finish your day visualizing the same goal. Soon this visualization will internalize and your subconscious will accept it as reality even though it doesn't exist yet. In chapter six, I stated that the subconscious can't differentiate between what's real and what's imagined. So as we impress this image of what we want to achieve, over time we reprogram our subconscious and it will move to create in our external environment what we imagined in the internal environment.

Everything that we wish for first has to be clearly defined and accepted internally before it can exist externally. This is such a beautiful principle. It clearly shows us how we have co-creative abilities by using our mind. We want to make sure from this point forward that our dominant thoughts are what we want and not what we don't want. I want to emphasize the word dominant. I have seen countless instances when people had bursts of good productive thought but lived in a negative and self-destructive way most of the time. Yet they believed that their dominant thoughts were the productive ones.

For example, about a month ago I had lunch with someone whom I haven't seen for a little while. During our meeting, this individual carried the conversation complaining about everything and anything, explaining to me why everything happening was all wrong. This went on for nearly an hour before he finally asked me what I thought. I told him that I wasn't concerned about any of the issues he brought up; my thoughts are purely on delivering what I need to do and I always look for the good in every situation. This person then told me he is like that too! You see, he thinks he is positive and solution-oriented but not once during the conversation did he say anything that would indicate that was, in fact, the case. Be honest with yourself as to what your dominant thoughts really are. Changing your thoughts from the negative to the positive is so easy if you find a goal that excites you. Every time you find yourself in a negative mindset, think about that wonderful exciting goal. As you begin thinking about it, your thoughts will switch to the 'how' side of the ledger.

Defining the big, exciting goals that we are emotionally attached to with constant visualization will internalize them. To actually achieve them, we need to take effective actions. Although nobody can reliably estimate how long the achievement of a goal will take, one thing is for certain. The more effective actions we take early in the process will allow us to achieve things as quickly as we can. Make every day count. One good practice is to have a notepad on the night table and before going to sleep. Write down the six most important things that need to be done the next day. Personally, I make a list for both my professional and personal goals. Writing them down allows the mind to think about how to complete these deliverables the next day; it also relaxes me as the next day is already defined so I can begin when I wake up. We won't need to worry in the morning about what we need to do that day or feel overwhelmed that we have no plan for all the tasks. As we wake up, our mind already knows what to do and will spend the day achieving these tasks and moving forward. Following these steps will increase productivity and the results will be apparent to everyone, including you.

In a previous chapter, we covered human actualization at a high level. We focused on personal growth and the importance of improving our understanding, knowledge and awareness. Most of you reading this book are either professionals or trained in some sort of business discipline. You have special skills that only people in your line of work are trained to have. What you do is important, and what will determine your level of success to a large extent will be your ability to accomplish those tasks. In fact, your compensation will be a direct reflection of the demand for the work you do, your ability to do it, and the difficulty in replacing you.

A very good way of increasing your skill level is by constantly learning about your profession. Some vocations require lifelong learning and this is a good thing. Most people, however, stop studying once they complete their schooling and thus their skills languish almost before they are fully put to use. I ask you once again to reflect on your activities and see how many nonfiction books you read over the last five years. Ask your friends, family and associates how many they read. You will find once again that this number won't be very large, so if you would like to accelerate your progress and achievements in your chosen field, dedicate some of your time to enhance your education, both professionally and personally. Even if you read only two pages per day and only during week days with a two-week holiday, you will still end up reading a total of five hundred pages per year. That volume of information could be two text books per annum.

This is far more than what most people do and gives you an advantage. Reading only two pages per day will require very little time and won't be overwhelming. It will be very easy to absorb the material and really try to understand and internalize it. It won't take long before you will be considered a very knowledgeable individual amongst your peers and co-workers. You will soon become an expert in your line of work, to such an extent that opportunities will open up one after the other and you will become an invaluable member of your organization. Your compensation will reflect that. You won't do this to compete against others, but to enhance your own capabilities and the outcome will be your improved standing, no matter the business sector.

Having very productive days consistently will result in increased contribution to your employer, company, profession, family or humanity in general. There is a law of polarity that states that everything has an equal and opposite side. For example, just as the sun sets it must rise, and just as there is bad in the world, there is also good in equal measure. Everything is in balance and you can't have one without the other. In physics we learn about cause and effect which is effectively the same thing. Every force has an opposite and equal force. When there is a cause there will be an equal effect. As we want more out of life instead of focusing on receiving, we need to spend our days on what we are giving and this in turn will give us what we want.

By maintaining our focus on giving, creating value and generally moving things forward and making things better, we will have no choice but the get the equal amount of reward for our contribution. The most common reward is money. Money itself is a medium of exchange and the reward for services rendered. I have heard so many times that people want more money, but seldom do I hear them say what additional contribution or value they are providing in order to earn the extra income they seek. As we give and create as much value as we possibly can each and every day, we will receive the rewards for our services as the result. We will also feel a lot better about ourselves. This progressive realization of our goals will make us successful and will give us a real sense of achievement. It will show us that yes, in fact, we are in control and can achieve almost anything we set our mind to.

Another law of life is the law of sacrifice. What this means is that if we want to get something of a higher value we need to give up something of a lower value. This law applies to all facets of our lives and its one we can all easily understand. For example when it comes to time, we know that there is no void in life; we fill up each minute possible. But if we want to achieve something more, then something must go. We don't get more time in each day, so we must prioritize and choose. For example, to continue reading and learning, or researching who we are and what we want will take time.

To do all these things, we won't get more time. We already have all the time possible – twenty-four hours each day – so we will need to give up things we currently do that may not be very important in order to free up some time to spend on these higher value activities.

Often these non-important activities become routine and it will seem that we already do all we can do because we are so busy. And it is true. We all spend every minute of our available time with something. The question is then, how valuable are these activities that we do? Should we continue doing them, or perhaps we could do away with some and utilize that time for better activities.

Some years ago, I had a strong urge to go outside. I was always inside all the time and was sick of it. I was inside my house, then the train, then my office, then the classroom, then the train, and then my house and this cycle repeated itself every day. I needed a change.

After some consideration, my family and I ended up choosing fishing as an outdoor family activity and something fun we could do together. So we got the required licenses, the tent, the fishing equipment, the portable barbeque, and we spent many weekends by the river and lakes near where we live. It was so refreshing and we all enjoyed it very much. As my girls grew older, going fishing wasn't as interesting of an activity for them anymore. Eventually I ended up just going myself.

It was still very nice being out in nature, and if I managed to catch something it was a bonus. It didn't take long before I became addicted to the activity and when I couldn't go, I watched shows on the fishing channel. I got so into it, for example, that during the winter months when fishing was not possible, I watched the shows sitting in the living room with a fishing rod in my hand. This of course was very entertaining for my family as you might well imagine. I still like fishing and have every intention of going again, but learning about the mind and writing this book was much more important to me so I set aside fishing for a while. I haven't had a rod in my hand for some time and I haven't watched fishing shows for many months now, either. I sacrificed fishing, which was my very enjoyable hobby, to do something that is far more important to me. You can do the same, I am sure. You just have to be willing to prioritize the things you want to achieve.

Another way of freeing up precious time is by utilizing it better. Commuting to my office in the morning and back home at night takes about two and a half hours out of my days. Instead of sitting on the train looking out of the window or closing my eyes to rest a bit more, I either listen to lectures on my IPod or read books that increase my awareness and enhance my skills in some way. Doing so ensures that this time is not wasted. It is also very common that parents take their children to activities like swimming lessons, or perhaps team sports like hockey or soccer. There is really no reason that, during these activities, a parent couldn't listen to lectures or read books that are designed to enhance their lives.

Lastly, let's talk about watching TV. It's a very big business with a lot of smart people constantly thinking about how to keep you in front of the tube. Sitting down in front of it is so easy, but getting up and walking away is very hard, even when you know it isn't benefiting you. TV executives know what they are doing and they know how to keep you captivated by their programs for hours. They, of course, work very closely with marketing executives, creating commercials showing you all the wonderful products you could buy from them while you are in a very receptive state. Some people get so into watching shows that it becomes part of who they are. Sometimes, when I hear people talk about last night's episode, it is almost as if they live their life through the shows they watch. They can't wait for the next episode to find out what will a certain character do as a result of another character saying something to somebody else. I wonder if those that get so into a show realize that what they see is fiction. Perhaps they pay more attention to this fantasy than managing and making their own life better. Don't be one of them. Pay attention to your own life, to your dreams and aspirations. You only live once, so you must get the most out of it. Enjoy this wonderful journey; enjoy as much as you can from the vast array of beautiful things life can offer. Utilize your time and your actions effectively and sacrifice the activities in your life that are of a lower value. Focus on the activities that are higher value that will allow you to achieve your dreams.

Continue your journey, explore your capabilities and understand how wonderful you really are. Don't stop learning. Take courses, read additional books, attend seminars and seek out the company of those individuals who can further enhance your understanding on this subject of the mind and your untapped potential. If you do that on a continual basis, you will amaze yourself at the improvements you will make. In no time you will need binoculars to look back to where you once were, and that is a very good thing!

Why Not?

Chapter 9

Living the Dream

Why Not?

Chapter 9

Living the Dream

You have read about many of life's true principles that will impact your life in a positive way if you adopt them. None of these principles are new or were invented by me. I have learned them from many life teachers and have used them effectively myself. These principles work for everyone the same way regardless of their age, sex or race. They work whether you accept their existence or not and whether you believe in them or not. They are universal and work every time without fail. If everything you have read so far made perfect sense to you and you can relate to these ideas, then you can clearly see how they will benefit you.

Once these principles became part of my habitual thinking, I got excited about what they could do for me and I developed a real sense of urgency to change. I have read countless books, listened to numerous lectures and completed a number of formal training programs. I love the subject of the mind and what we can achieve through maximizing our own human potential, and wanted to become the product of these ideas at the earliest possible time. I was anxious and in a hurry.

Then I learned that 'hurry' is not a good thing. To efficiently work with life's principles I had to relax, and calm down, but at the same time increase my effectiveness and intensity. You see, when we rush, we apply force, and using force never leads to long term benefit. We are merely busier instead of being 'on purpose.' As a starting point, I needed to strengthen my mind and use my will to control my thoughts. Then, using this newly gained skill, I focused my attention on improving myself one step and one lesson at a time. I needed to learn that since I now have the user manual for life, or the keys to the kingdom, I don't need to hurry any more.

Instead of being in a hurry, I must do the best I can to complete the most important tasks each day. That is what makes the difference. It is not the volume of things I do, but the importance, the quality of my work and how I do it.

The creative process, when we develop something that hasn't existed before, will require time. We can't control how long things will take; we can only estimate and keep trying. With practice we can estimate fairly accurately but never with certainty. We shouldn't even attempt to control the length of time, and should instead focus on the end result and take positive actions every day toward the achievement of that goal. Relax and know that the day will come when everything you want will be realized.

Awareness is the foundation of growth, whether it is a personal or a professional matter. Not understanding how something works, what influences the outcome, or how to modify the process to achieve the desired end state, makes it impossible to manage whatever issue we are dealing with. This principle applies in the same way to a computer program as to our own mind. Just as you can't correct or fix a bug in software if you don't understand the underlying code, you can't fix the results in your life if you don't understand the thought process that brought those results into being.

The two best ways to increase our awareness is study and meditation. I highly recommend doing both. Earlier, I suggested you read nonfiction books to increase your knowledge (awareness) of your chosen profession or whatever subject of interest you wish to pursue. You know how important it is to understand the mind, so I am sure you will seek ways to learn more about it too.

Meditation has been a big part of Eastern cultures for thousands of years and it is growing in its popularity in the West as well. There are various programs available, so starting one is not difficult and well worth the effort. During meditation we learn to relax our mind, giving it a much needed rest. By calming our mind, we also relax the body and the combination of the two provide rejuvenation. It is not unusual to feel better and more refreshed after an hour-long meditation then after getting a good night's sleep. This deep relaxation significantly reduces anxiety and fear.

The benefit of this calmer existence has a big impact on our physiology as well. The chemistry of the body changes from acidic (from stress) to alkaline and balanced. The body functions in a more natural way; it improves the weakened immune system and our health in general. You may remember my own mother's example when she fought cancer. The physiological and psychological benefits of mediation have been studied by many institutions as well as the medical profession and the benefits are well-documented, accepted and recognized. Though my mother's experience is anecdotal, it is still just as real. She now lives a wonderfully healed life and her new attitude and lifestyle was a big part of that healing.

During meditation, the focus is on our mental abilities such as monitoring our thoughts, gaining control over them and envisioning what we want. It helps to switch our thoughts from our external environment to inside our mind. Meditation also increases our mental abilities by harmonizing the two hemispheres of our brain. As you know, the brain has two sides, the left being the logical half and the right the emotional. Men tend to use their left hemisphere more while woman use predominantly their right. Each one is equally important and by harmonizing the two it creates a much higher level of awareness and allows us to function better in every way. This leads to what is called 'whole brain thinking.' It is generally accepted by scientists that we only use a small percentage of our brain for conscious thought. Imagine the impact it will have on your life when you have access to more and strive to use it.

I have been meditating for years and would not stop for any reason because it adds so much to my life. I think most people know how beneficial meditation is and also know someone who achieved great improvement as the result. Those who don't do it, despite knowing the benefits, may perhaps resist because of a perceived lack of available time. If you are one of these people, I would ask you to give meditation a chance and see what happens. I sure am happy that I did. It didn't take long for me to see and feel the improvements in every area of my life. I enjoyed how I became a calmer, more relaxed and more capable individual – so much so that continuing the meditation was not only easy, but natural.

We have covered many subjects in this text, including meditation, and incorporating them into your everyday life may seem too much to handle, especially all at once. If you feel this way that is okay, because it means you are growing and you want yourself to stretch and imagine a different life. You understand the changes you need to make and why, and you are peeking outside the box. Feeling uncomfortable with information that is new is perfectly natural; in fact, it is a built in function we have because our minds want to keep the status quo.

Evolving into a higher existence will require changing the way you think. Modifying your value sets and your translation of how life works can be a very difficult, seemingly impossible task. How much of an effort it will take is simply a function of the level of your resistance. The choice is yours and the perception of it being 'easy' or 'hard' is purely yours. This, again, is really good news because it means that you are in charge and if your transformation is a difficult one, you can choose to make it easier. The control is with you.

We have discussed how easy it is to change our thoughts, and how our thoughts create our feelings. These then determine our actions and, of course, our actions create results. A good way to take control of your life is by paying attention to your feelings. When you feel good, notice how everything seems to be coming along great, everything is effortless, right on target and good all around. When you have these emotions, observe your thoughts. You will find that you are at ease with what is happening around you and you appreciate everything you see and experience. On the other hand, when you feel bad, your thoughts will be limiting in nature. Be aware that when you have bad feelings, you are in a negative vibration, thinking negative thoughts. When you are feeling this way, you are resisting something, whether it is real or imagined. I believe that nobody likes to feel bad. We all prefer to feel good. This is why we need to take charge and change this negative feeling into a good one as soon as possible.

In order to change your thoughts, it helps to look at yourself as an observer might. Don't judge or force; simply relax and observe those thoughts flying through the screen of your mind. Ask questions like: What am I resisting? What am I upset about? You may find that what created the bad feeling is unimportant, or is a reaction from the past that is long gone. You may be worrying about something that hasn't even happened yet. Few things that cause an emotional reaction will be real and current. As you discover what is happening in your mind during these periods, you are raising your awareness and identifying issues. As you become cognizant of these, you will gain the ability to ignore them or set them aside when they arise. As you exercise your reasoning faculty to reject and/or neglect those negative thoughts and then choose more productive ones instead you gain control over them. You will soon realize that a lot of what happens in the screen of your mind is uninvited and unnecessary and to entertain those thoughts is a complete waste of time. It won't take long before you will be able to say, "Get out of here!" and move on to thoughts that serve you.

A practical application of this would be, for example, if you had a meeting during the day that didn't go particularly well. Perhaps people made you look bad and didn't appreciate the work you did. This experience may stick with you for the rest of the day, a week or if very traumatic, even years. You may replay in your mind everything that happened repeatedly, telling yourself how wrong those people were and allowing yourself to relive the anger. These negative thoughts will be your dominant ones and will make you feel bad as long as you don't eliminate or replace them. Realize that the past can't be changed, what happened already happened, and instead of thinking about how wrong people in that meeting were, start to look forward instead. You can start to think about how to manage such a meeting better next time, how to show your good work more effectively, how to get more work done and better, how to gain confidence and the respect of those who matter. By doing this, you will not only start to feel better, but will actually work on productive activities that create value, move things forward, and make life better. I am sure you see that choosing these new thoughts will have a positive impact and rather than brewing in the past.

It sounds easy and it is. I do it every day. With practice, it will become easier and easier. The key is gaining awareness of what we are thinking about and what is that we are resisting. With practice, it will come naturally and effortlessly. What will also happen is the realization that by not controlling and eliminating these bad thoughts, you really are only hurting yourself. You have no effect on the people that attended that meeting. It is ancient history to them. As soon as you realize this, taking charge and focusing on what works for you becomes much easier and fun. Over time, as you leave more and more in the past and take charge of your thoughts, your mind won't allow you to sabotage yourself. The bad habits and thoughts will fall by the wayside and will be replaced with more productive thoughts and actions that serve you and make your life better.

Another reason you may feel bad is because your conditioning has a very strong hold on you. Your internal map of reality is firmly implanted in your mind especially when you are influenced by something (perhaps my book!) that entices you to question and change your thoughts and behaviour. Realize that doing things that you are not accustomed to can make you temporarily feel bad as well, because it conflicts with the way you have been thinking and living. Again, awareness is the key in understanding where this emotion is coming from and why.

Understand that discomfort is natural and a given in the process of increasing your awareness and evolving your thinking, habits and paradigms to a higher level. If you find that a bad feeling is the result of internalizing a new and better way of thinking or doing effective actions that you are not accustomed to doing, realize that this will actually feel good in the long run. It means that you are evolving. You are rearranging and reworking your internal map of reality and it will allow you to have a more prosperous and joyful life.

Over time you will get comfortable with being un-comfortable. As you stay with this new activity or way of thinking you grow into a higher level of awareness and this higher level will become your new norm. What seemed like a big thing before will no longer require attention and will become an obvious, natural part of living. The bad feeling will disappear and you will experience a sense of peace and happiness. It will be almost like when you arrive at the end of a journey. Once you get to this new level of awareness and your horizon expands you will realize that there are even better ways of thinking and doing and you will be ready to grow again. With that, the whole cycle will start over again.

I could cite a hundred examples of uncomfortable issues I had to overcome as part of my studies and, while I don't want to bore you with all of them, there is one that you need to know about. As a student of this material, one of the first lessons I learned was that I am in full charge of my life and anything that happened to me and will happen to me. I need to take 100 percent responsibility for everything in my life. For me, this was a difficult thing to accept. First, it didn't seem reasonable. I didn't think it was true at all. I firmly believed in looking at my external circumstances as real and uncontrollable. Looking back, I had a victim mentality.

At the beginning I didn't understand how the external is simply a reflection of my internal thoughts – it was a bit confusing. I also didn't comprehend how, with my thoughts, I created my present and also my future. But they are both true statements and are key parts of the creative process. As I learned these principles, the uncomfortable feeling of being in charge and realizing the mistakes I made were my doing faded away and were replaced with joy and happiness. It feels so good to know that it really is up to me to live the life I want. The idea that I am in charge, am in control, and can achieve what I want feels fantastic.

An essential part of developing a positive mental state is by having an attitude of gratitude. Remember what you learned in physics class. A body in motion remains in motion until an outside force counters it.

What this means is that if you are grateful for all the things you have in your life - even for things that you haven't achieved or received yet - you will attain more to be grateful for. The reality is that we have so much good in our life that it would take a long time to write down all the things for which we could be, and should be, grateful. Having running water, electricity, transportation, food, bank accounts and many other things that we take for granted everyday is a blessing.

Look around and think about how life would be if you didn't have all that you enjoy today. It's the simple things we take for granted. What would you do if you didn't have comfortable chairs? How different would life be if we didn't have computers or cars? Sure, they may break down from time to time and cause you hardship, but life would be so much more difficult without them. Let's be grateful for all the good we have attained so far. We have so much to be thankful and grateful for. Let's not take anything for granted or look at it from a negative perspective, let's appreciate it instead.

One common thing for people to complain about is paying bills. Instead of getting frustrated about them piling up, when you pay them practice feeling the joy of the benefits you received, and paying for the services for which you are grateful. So when you get your electrical bill, realize how much better your life is that the electricity powers your refrigerator, your air conditioning, your washer and dryer. Be thankful that you don't need to wander around the house in the dark, or depend on candles, because you have light even when it is dark outside. In North America, having a car is almost a must, especially in the suburbs and rural areas. Paying the monthly payments, the insurance, the fuel and the upkeep can really add up, no doubt. But imagine what your life would be like if you had to take public transportation everywhere and were limited by those schedules and constraints rather than having the freedom to just hop in your car anytime day or night and go where ever you want. Paying your bills is one way to practice your new grateful attitude. As you learn to see the good in every area you have previous disliked or dreaded, your perspective will change.

This attitude of gratitude must also include ourselves and others as well. We are such marvellous creatures with unlimited potential and co-creative capabilities. We can achieve so much. We can make such a difference in the quality of other peoples' lives. We can be a positive influence to those in our circle, those in our town and then even to millions by sharing what we have learned. It's in all of us to do good and it feels great. That positive boost we get from helping others helps us, too. By focusing on those outside ourselves, we aren't dwelling on what problems we have, and in fact, we often realize how much harder others have it than we do. It is a good reminder to be grateful and give back whenever we can.

It is also important to know that we all have the same capabilities regardless of sex, age or race. The difference between two people is not what they are capable of, but only their level of awareness. As you meet with people, remember that this is another marvellous creature and as such, should be treated with the utmost respect. This also applies to the workplace, especially if you are a manager. Treat each individual you deal with on a daily basis as if they are the most important person in the whole world, because it is true. Make eye contact and listen to what they have to say. Don't stare at your phone or read email or be distracted in any way because that sends the message that they are unimportant, even if that is not your intention.

If you reflect on your life, you must have had at least one instance, and probably more, where someone saw the wonders in your potential and was not shy about telling you. They talked to you in a way that reflected their sincere belief about how amazing you are. I bet you can remember those moments. Perhaps it was a parent, a teacher, a boss or even a spouse. It is interesting that we remember those people because this kind of reinforcement occurs so rarely. You remember their name, the place you met and the circumstance. You remember everything about what they said and you think about those moments with joy.

Everyone you will meet with will have good qualities. See, recognize and acknowledge these good qualities out loud. Don't keep it to yourself. Years from now, that person may remember that one moment with happiness and joy, so don't miss the chance to share something positive. Let them know that you see the good in them, but make sure you mean it. Flattery is hollow and unproductive. Be sincere and honest. It is easy, because you know it is true. What may be hard is changing your habitual interactions to focus on the good in people instead of on the things that you may think bother you about them. Focus on those good qualities and help them evolve even further.

It is a good goal to leave everyone you meet with an aura of increase. This means they feel better for having known or met you. People naturally want to grow and always like to associate themselves with those who exude positivity. The person who helps them evolve will always be in demand. Managers and leaders should take special note. Being a leader is about inspiring the team and bringing out the best, not managing processes. Countless times a good worker becomes a manager and in the new role they focus on managing the processes instead of bringing the best out of the team. It's easy to focus on numbers or tasks, but much harder to choose to be involved with people. Emotions are messy, but we must understand how those emotions can help or hurt the workplace before we can start inspiring people.

Show your appreciation for others and you will radiate love and compassion at all times. People will sense the positive vibration coming from you and will want to be around you. Think about the people in your life right now that you really love to be around. Do they exude positive energy? Odds are they do and that is what makes you want to spend time with them. Every time you leave their presence you feel happy. What you put out will always come back. When you treat people with the utmost respect and appreciation they will treat you exactly the same way. You know the difference between an environment where people appreciate and like each other versus one where there is dislike and distrust.

Take charge and be the positive force. Don't wait for others to start. Be the first and you will be amazed at how quickly things will improve. Oftentimes people hold off and are unwilling to take the first step until someone else takes it for them, which of course never works – you end up waiting for a 'right time' that never comes.

If you think back to the law of cause and effect, you know that nothing will change until you start taking action to make it change. You should want to be the cause that eventually brings on the effect of a more pleasant environment. Have something nice to say to people, even if it is just a small thing. Everyone likes a compliment and it makes the receiver feel good and worthy of notice, but the funny thing is that it also makes the giver feel good too.

The Body is Important Too

As we have discussed, the mind is infinitely more important than the body and this book is focused on understanding and utilizing the mind. However, this book would not be complete if some critical issues were not mentioned in relation to the body as it is the external shell that everyone sees.

Our society focuses way too much on the physical part of our being – to the exclusion of the mind. Looks are so important for many that some even dedicate most of their lives to always looking the best and at times forget that real beauty comes from the inside. You know how popular plastic surgery is, and how fake some physical beings become. Real beauty radiates from the soul. When the mind is together, the body is together. But when the body is the starting point and little or no emphasis is spent on the inner self, beauty becomes skin deep and personalities very shallow. It will fade and require constant surgical intervention, but it will always remain skin deep unless the spiritual side is also well-tended.

Don't take me wrong, I, like everybody else, appreciate things that are pleasing to my eyes, but I also know that my vision is only one of my senses and what I see isn't that important at the end of the day. I also firmly believe that the vessel we have needs to be taken care of. The body we get, whether we like it or not, is what we have to work with and we will have to live with it until our last breath. We may not like our skin color, our height, the shape of our body, or a myriad of other physical attributes, but the reality is that this is what we have and we need to take good care of it. Of course the focus of this book is the mind, but there are several critical things we can do physically to help our minds function better and help us feel better.

The first of these is motion. Our body was designed to move, but modern life involves a lot of sitting and there are many people with very little physical activity (like me—right now). I'm sitting in my office and the only things moving are my fingers as I write this chapter.

This isn't nearly enough activity for the hours I've been sitting here. We all need to get in the habit of moving in some way or form. It doesn't have to include a gym membership, but perhaps you could take ballroom dancing classes with your partner or walks on the beach or around the neighbourhood. It doesn't need to be extensive, but it should be regular and enjoyable.

Exercise produces endorphins which elevate our mood and this helps us keep our mind focused on the positive. It also keeps illness at bay and keeps our weight in check. When you are ill, or feel very overweight, it is extremely difficult to maintain a positive mindset because you are faced with pain, or more external negativity. Health and happiness go hand in hand, so I would be remiss if I didn't include some comments to this effect. You can choose to feel better physically and that will assist in your efforts to control your thoughts.

Another area we need to take very seriously is what we eat. There are many studies showing how depleted the soil has become over the years, producing food that is lacking in minerals and vitamins. As I grew up in Hungary, most of the things we consumed were locally produced and sustainable, made in a way that we now call organic. The food had great flavour, texture, and real substance. Because of that, people ate a lot less as their body got what it needed in a more concentrated form. I remember so many people had chickens and other fowls and some even had pigs, goats, or sheep on their land.

Some of you may find this a bit rural or an ancient way to live but the fact is that all of that was real and in truth was a better way to eat and live than many people do now. Even nowadays when I visit my parents and my mother cooks for me, the chicken we eat comes from one of their friends. The meat is darker and tougher, but so much more flavourful. It never ceases to amaze me how different it is compared to the fluffed, antibiotic injected, cage raised "rubber" chicken I buy in my local supermarket. When I eat what my mother makes, eating just one piece makes me full and content, but at home I can eat the whole grilled 'rubber' chicken from the supermarket and despite feeling like I will explode, I still crave more. You see, when the food contains enough minerals, vitamins and enzymes, our body knows when to stop and we don't end up eating more calories than we need. When we eat the 'rubber' chicken or other products, we end up eating unneeded chemicals, but we also eat a whole lot more calories. We are getting a huge array of empty calories without the necessary nutritional content.

Fruits are another noticeable issue. I love strawberries, but am always disappointed when I eat them here in Toronto. They all look perfect, large and appetizing, but they barely have any smell or taste. It's like I am eating watery fluff and get pretty much nothing out of it. But if you pick on right off the plant in a home garden, the taste is so much more vibrant and satisfying. Growing your own food, or sourcing it from a local organic farm, can go a long way toward a healthier more satisfied life.

Most of us, including me, have gone through the drive through on the way home so we don't have to cook. We all do this occasionally, but there are many people for whom this is a way of life. You have no idea what is really in fast food, and invariably you feel bad afterword. I'm not starting a crusade against fast food, I'm only saying that the choices you make in what you consume matters. It matters in how you feel, how you act and how your treat others. If you're tired or not feeling good from that big burger you ate a lunch, then you are going to say and do things you might not otherwise if you felt better.

We'd like to think that things like this really don't matter – but they do. It is important to take care of yourself in the best way possible. It is essential that your body gets the fuel it needs to function at the optimal level and that you not stuff yourself with junk. I said a few times before that we are marvellous creatures and it is so true. Scientists and the medical community have been studying our bodies for centuries and they still don't fully understand how it works. When it gets what it needs it can heal many illnesses on its own, without chemical or medicinal intervention. I am a firm believer that we are on the verge of a wellness revolution and as more and more people realize that living in the microwave society has its drawbacks and start to take care of their bodies by exercising and eating better, we will see a significant reduction in illnesses and diseases.

I purposefully ended the last paragraph with the word disease. The reason for that is that our body is the manifestation of our mind and our thoughts. It's no secret that stress has a significant effect on our health, but what we must understand is that stress is self-induced and can be eliminated by proper control and usage of our mind. No doctor or scientist would dispute the link between the mind and the impact it has on the body.

When you have an illness you have a disease. It is 'Dis Ease.' This means your mind is not at ease and since it is full of unwanted, negative, and unproductive thoughts, it will manifest itself in your body which produces a 'not at ease' state or a Dis-Ease. So make sure you know and manage what is happening in your mind because it impacts the body in tremendous ways. This temporary vessel for your soul may not be around for too long if you don't take care of it.

Why Not?

Chapter 10

Self Rescue for Beginners

Why Not?

Chapter 10

Self Rescue for Beginners

There will be events or even entire stages of life that you will prefer not to experience. Some of these will be inevitable, while others can be avoided or their impact minimized. Life has a natural rhythm to it and the balance between negative events and positive ones does exist. So when you have joyful times, you need to know and expect that there will be moments when you will have to utilize your intellectual faculties to overcome whatever life throws your way that might be negative. Know that challenges will come and your experience in life will depend on your ability to overcome them.

Perhaps the most traumatic of all these challenges is the loss of a loved one. We each will experience the passing of loved ones, some more and some less, as we grow and age. It is inevitable. Our body is not designed to live forever. Sooner or later, the day will come when it stops functioning and will no longer be the vessel for our soul. Nobody knows when this day will come and, while most people live a long life, others are taken from us without warning and way too early. These can be the most devastating. No matter how it occurs, loss is always shocking. Even if someone has experienced significant health challenges and has been hospitalized in intensive care for an extensive period, it doesn't make the experience any easier. I remember so clearly one morning a few years ago, coming to work to find all my team members in total shock and disbelief. Our manager, our friend, had passed the previous night in his very early forties, leaving his loving wife and children behind. It was so sudden and very sobering to think that one minute you are laughing and going about your world and the next minute you are gone.

When we experience such a traumatic experience, it jolts us and makes us realize that we ourselves are vulnerable and we have no guarantee of tomorrow. We may think we will live forever but nobody knows how much time we have left. We make commitments to ourselves about spending more time with the family, improving our human relationships and taking better care of our bodies. Even with the best of intentions, most people lose the desire to carry out their own commitment within days. Once the initial shock is gone, people tend to fall back into their old ways. Their well-ingrained habits continue controlling every aspect of their lives and they fall right back into their routine.

In a strange way, I consider myself fortunate that I have attended literally hundreds of funerals. You recall I played music from an early age and, as a teenager, was a member of the marching band in the small mining town where I grew up. Our band was funded by the coal mine and, in return, we played on festive events but also at funerals. Mining isn't the safest occupation and there were quite a few people that made it to work okay in the morning but never came back home. People like that were often the parents of my friends and it was hard to watch them suffer. Because it was a small town, most people knew each other and often were either closely or distantly related, so more often than not we knew the person and the family involved.

In the army, I was also a member of the marching band and, as you might guess, we played at countless funerals.

The big difference between what happened in my old town versus in the army was that, in the army, we usually didn't know the person whose funeral we attended.

I can tell you with certainty that despite all these experiences, I never grew totally immune to becoming emotional at these events. What has changed is how I handle the experience. It is much easier for me now than how it was at the beginning. Throughout my life, I have come to accept that the human body won't live forever. I also learned and accepted that it really is not the body we need to focus on, but the soul - the mind. The body is really just a mere reflection of our spiritual being. We are not our body; we just live there. We are, at the end of the day, spirits living in a body. The body really is just a mere vessel making us visible to others and allowing us to physically move things around. This body is finite and limited, but the soul is limitless and infinite.

Knowing and really understanding that we are spiritual beings results in our changed view about life – and death. Those who focus on the body pay attention to the less important and miss appreciating and recognizing what really matters. You see, the way I learned to handle the passing of a friend or a loved one is by knowing that their spirit lives on. The body may have stopped functioning, but what made our relationship special was the soul. Instead of focusing on the ending of the physical relationship, I focus on the good memories, the joy, the laughs, and the achievements the person made. I also know that their spirit will always be with us. Friendships and partnerships are the result of two souls resonating together or existing in harmony. When this harmony is strong, some people even refer to is as being soul mates.

Based on this spiritual foundation, another way I changed was by appreciating every day and everybody. I see the good in people, I see the wonders and possibilities and I celebrate them. I have seen people with regrets think about how they should have done things better had they known the end was near. Well, you know right now that the end is coming, you just don't know when. Why not treat each other as related spirits, kindred and offspring of the deathless soul right now, and tomorrow, and the day after that, and every day going forward? Let us put our perceived differences aside and celebrate the company of everyone we come into contact with every day. When the final hour arrives, instead of regrets and bad memories, we can celebrate the journey we enjoyed together and know that nothing and nobody can take those away from us.

A very good way to look at the impact someone made on the life of others is by looking at the legacy they leave behind. It has become more important to me than ever to leave a legacy. Who wants to exist on this earth – perhaps for eight or nine decades only to be forgotten the second you pass?

Impacting the lives of many in a very positive manner, and generally being regarded as someone who worked toward something meaningful that he was passionate about, is how I would like people to remember me. I want them to know that I impacted their lives in a positive and lasting manner. This is not to gain glory for myself, but to know that these principles that changed my life are still going and changing others' lives far into the future.

There are cultures around the world where instead of feeling the sorrow, the people celebrate the passing of their friend and loved one. They celebrate the good and that the spirit is now reunited with its Maker. I think we can all learn from that and understand that it is a natural part of living – not something horrible that is sent along to try our souls.

You will also experience many other forms of setbacks and challenges in your life that can threaten to derail your growth. They come in various forms and events. Some people break their family union and go separate ways, some lose their jobs, some lose their savings, some deal with chronic illness – the list is almost endless. In fact, there will be no shortage of challenges and most people will experience a wide variety and possibly experience the same type of event multiple times. How many people do you know that have been married multiple times or who have lost many loved ones, or suffered an endless barrage of financial problems? This is just another fact of life.

Instead of getting bogged down by these events and feeling sorry for ourselves, we need to focus on how to handle them. As we face each new challenge, we must ask what changes we need to make to still achieve our desires, goals and aspirations. Those who know exactly what they want and why they want it find it easier to handle setbacks than those who don't. Setbacks and getting off course are quite normal but only your character will determine if you allow them to convince you to give up or keep going.

The two most common setbacks people experience are divorce and losing a job. Divorce is rather frequent in western society and is an acceptable way of resolving issues between couples. Despite it being a frequently occurring situation, it is always a difficult challenge to go through. Over the years a lot of memories are built together, children became part of the family and financial obligations are made. Breaking up this family union is a difficult decision and a trying process. I am not a marriage counsellor and would not make any recommendations to anyone about how to handle their marital problems, but even during a stressful time such as this, you can choose how you respond.

Remember that we are all related souls. Even if your spouse did things that made it unbearable for you to stay in the relationship, forgive them. Forgive them for not knowing better or for not choosing better and allow yourself to put the marriage in the past if that is your choice. Forgive yourself, too. It is quite natural for anybody in this situation to do some 'soul-searching,' analyze the situation, and potentially discovering many things that they themselves could have done much better. It is always easy to be smart after the fact, so don't be too harsh on yourself. Accept that what happened has already happened. Learn from the mistakes but stop reliving them. Treat your former partner with the utmost respect regardless of what happened between the two of you and move on. Know and believe that you are a worthy person and deserve to create a wonderful relationship with another like-minded soul. Go about your days with a clear vision of what you want, including the loving relationship you desire and your future partner will one day come your way.

Losing a job is also quite common, especially in today's economy. Companies manage their human resources much more dynamically than ever and this often includes large scale layoffs. The investment community demands performance quarter by quarter and the leaderships responsibility is to deliver acceptable returns for the shareholders. To meet the demands of the investment, leaders frequently adjust the workforce to the changing market conditions. At times, whole divisions are shut down, and complete teams and groups disappear from one day to the next. Downsizing is also a cleansing process where underperformers are asked to leave, making room for a higher potential individual to join the organization. Either way, losing your livelihood is never a pleasant experience. But it could be a catalyst for a wonderful next phase. There are countless examples of when someone lost their job, but instead of immediately taking another one, decided to take some time for self-reflection and self-searching. Armed with this newly found understanding of likes and dislikes, they were then able to land a position that was far more suitable. When a person's desires match the demand of the role, magic happens. The choice is always there. Should I panic and take the first job I can get, or should I understand myself better first and get a job that makes me really happy? You know the answer to this dilemma but it's not always an easy choice.

Another point that loss of income highlights is the need for multiple sources of income. Throughout our history the wealthy always had multiple sources of income. In fact, to become wealthy, it is almost a prerequisite. I think anybody who believes financial independence is a state that we should all achieve must take this idea seriously. When you have, let's say five or ten different income sources available, it's not only that your income is much higher than would be otherwise, but it also creates income stability. If one source is not coming along that well, the others could easily supplement. It also provides a lot of safety and reduces anxiety over money. Those who have multiple sources of income stop working for money - they work for the enjoyment of doing what they like to do and getting paid is a bonus.

There are many different sources of income available, especially via the internet, as you can use your skills to teach others or offer seminars or even write a book. The more you have going, the less vulnerable you are to a layoff or a big employer that decides to close your division. Does it take time to cultivate these sources? Without a doubt. But again, you have to ask yourself if you really want it. If you do, you will prioritize those goals and fit them into your life.

People who don't have a clear vision of their future generally find it harder to deal with difficulties. Without a clear end result they aren't really sure what adjustment they need to make. I have seen people carry a burden and hold onto something in the past for a long period of time. Sometimes they feel what happened impacted them in such a profound way that they just simply can't move on. This of course is not true, even if it seems so at the time. We always have a choice. We have full control over our thoughts - thoughts will create our feelings, feelings spark our actions, and those actions create our results.

I have heard some people, who experienced something extremely traumatic in their past, say that I just don't understand or that I have no idea what it's like. These are both true, but I also know that they have choice to hang onto those events and refuse to let them go. Some people even treat their trauma like a security blanket and excuse for not living their dreams. If you need professional help to get past a traumatic event, then get it. If you choose to move forward, it will happen –but if you don't choose to, it never will.

Sometimes people deal with the setbacks by starting destructive behaviours. There is no shortage of those who find their refuge in the bottle, narcotics or other dangerous or addictive behaviour. Of course, none of these behaviours has ever solved anybody's problems. At best they create a new set of problems that have the potential to snowball into a series of other problems. The bottom line is that these behaviours are trying to cover or avoid the pain and it festers and builds. Eventually the emotions will rise to the surface and once they do you still have to deal with them or destroy yourself. Though it may hurt, it is much better to experience that hurt and grow from it, rather than cover it up or put it off and then destroy your whole life. I have also heard people say that time will solve everything. Time will not solve anything at all. The only thing that can solve the problem is us and we must face challenges head on.

In order to get through those negative emotions, you must realize, understand and believe that you in fact can move on. It is often said that in order to recover you must first acknowledge the problem and that is what you are doing. You are realizing the problem is you and you have the power to fix it. You always have a choice of how to respond. Never react. Stop. Think. Respond.

Know, understand and believe that you become what you think about and nobody but you can choose your thoughts. You have full control over them. You can choose any thoughts you want and your thoughts will determine what your life is going to be like. A good way to change your dominant thoughts away from the sorrow or pain you are dealing with is by finding something that reignites your passion. For some it maybe a new hobby, for others it maybe a new business venture, travel or other achievements like mountain climbing. Find yours. Listen to your inner voice give you hint about this wonderful new passion and go for it. Immerse yourself in it and, as you get involved, a wonderful new world will unfold in front of your eyes. You will once again find your joy and happiness and those old limiting beliefs will no longer control you. This of course doesn't mean that you forget about what happened; it simply means that thoughts around it will no longer be your dominant thoughts and you can now move forward to greener pastures.

Study like you will live forever and live your life knowing that today maybe your last day - and never, never give up. There is always a tomorrow and you can have it all. Your best years are yet to come. Know that they will. It's only up to you.

Why Not?

Chapter 11

The Best is Yet to Come!

Why Not?

Chapter 11

The Best is Yet to Come!

I hope you enjoyed reading this book as much as I enjoyed writing it. As with many other things in life, writing a book is a journey of personal growth and I grew even as I wrote these pages. I do sincerely hope that there were many thoughts in the book that grabbed your attention and resonated with you.

You have probably heard the saying 'Repetition is the mother of all knowledge' and it is true. Repetition is essential to change your habitual ways of thinking and acting. The conditioning you now have was ingrained in your mind over the course of many years and those old ideas are well-entrenched. To replace them will take effort and time. Reading this book once will start to have an impact but to make it a lasting one, constant repetition of these concepts and an ongoing effort will be required to replace old habits in thought and action.

It won't take long at all and you will start to see the impact and the benefits reveal themselves. At that point, putting in more effort won't feel like any effort at all. It is not something you will have to do; it will be something you want to do.

The concepts covered in this book are time-tested and proven not only by me, but by countless others. They have always existed and many go back to the most ancient texts.

For all of human existence, they have worked uniformly for everyone without fail. We live in a very exact world and the laws described in the book are as functional as any of the laws in the physical sciences.

As I started to study this material, perhaps the most important message for me was that it is up to me. The past does not have to be an indication of my future. Those who are willing to learn, to understand themselves, and are willing to make the necessary changes, can significantly change the course of their lives. As J.D. Rhymes, the famous psychologist from the last century said, "The greatest discovery of our time is that human beings can alter their life by altering the attitude of their minds." Isn't that good news for us all?

So if your circumstances at the moment aren't what you would like to see, don't worry and don't settle. Your current circumstances are nothing more than the reflection of your thinking up until now. Change your thinking and this will result in changed feelings, changed actions and improved results. You are a co-creator and you can get what you want.

As you read this book, you read a great deal about me. You saw how many transformations I went through and how different a person I became over the years. You also saw that like many in my age group, midlife crises impacted me just as much as it impacts others. I'm not unique or different, but I was so happy to discover these laws and could hardly wait to implement them. I am so glad I did. It is difficult for me to describe how my life turned around. I used to be miserable and if I want to be honest with myself, not always easy to be around. I was snappy, frustrated, lost and directionless. Now if I think back to those years, I jokingly call them the 'lost years,' but I have no regrets. Every experience I had was essential in making me who I am today. If anything from my past was missing, I wouldn't be me. You see, I like me now. I am quite happy with who I am today and the things that I am creating in my life. I like everything about it. I love my life.

I now feel in full control; the past doesn't occupy my thoughts and the future looks really bright. I forgave myself and forgave everyone in my past. I hold no grudge and live my life in a way that allows every day to be a wonderful new beginning. I wake up with a smile on my face and am fulfilled and happy at night when I retire for the day. I know where I am heading, I can see my future very clearly and do everything I can each day to achieve this beautiful vision of mine. Having this 'user's manual' for life allowed me to regain complete control, tremendously improve my human relationships, and my financial circumstances, as well as my outlook on life. Some years ago I was wondering if what I had then was the most I would achieve; now I know that is not the case. I am just starting out. I am only about half way through and I am 100% convinced the best is yet to come in my life.

You can have this too. We are all equally capable and have the same potential. The choice is yours, whether you would like to significantly improve your life or continue on your current path. Whether your current path gives you what you want is something only you can decide. But I want to ask you to be totally honest with yourself and truly reflect on your life. Realize that your old conditioning will tell you, "this is all you can have and you should be grateful for it. Stop dreaming." But you don't have to listen to the old conditioning. Dream and imagine what your life would be like if you knew you couldn't fail. Use that as a measuring stick instead of those old negative thoughts.

Information contained in this book is invaluable in the corporate setting as well. To increase the efficiency of a department, let's say by ten percent, is not an easy or common task, but to increase an individual's effectiveness multiple times over, is relatively easy. I firmly believe that the next frontier in managing companies and organizations is the management of human capital. The management of their incredible talent. Companies can get a lot more done with a lot less if these resources are understood and well-utilized. When employees are happy, fulfilled, inspired and willingly to do what needs to be done, there will be a direct impact on the bottom line each and every day.

The rate of change we experienced over the last 150 years is nothing short of incredible. Remember, the driving force behind these changes was innovation and the first step in innovation is imagination. Imagining things that didn't exist before and making it a reality is what innovation is. So as this trend is continuing, we know that people will be using their imaginative faculties more and more. They will combine the imagination with the other intellectual faculties to deliver astonishing results. I would reason than that understanding how our mind works is of paramount importance.

Knowing that the rate of change is accelerating, I can't wait to see all the wonderful enhancements and improvements we will experience in our lives. But I don't want to be a passive observer. I want to be driving a lot of that change. I want to stay current and relevant and know that there is so much untapped potential in each of us to make quantum leaps in our results, which means our dreams are possible and attainable. My purpose is to help individuals and companies harness this power.

As a parting thought, I would like to emphasize that you should know, understand and believe that you have infinite potential in you and your life should be an absolute joyride each and every day. I urge you to continue your journey of self-discovery. I am also pleased and honoured to have shared my experiences with you and hope to have the opportunity to impact your company or your private life in a positive manner. Always hope, always dream and know that together, we are creating our bold new world.

Thank you

Attila Varga

CPSIA information can be obtained at www.ICGtesting.com
Printed in the USA
LVOW122351091112

306691LV00005B/1/P